ב"ה

Outsmarting Antisemitism

AUTHORS
Rabbi Baruch Shalom Davidson
Rabbi Lazer Gurkow
Rabbi Shmuel Super

Cover Art: *Leipzig Machzor* (detail), ca. 1300.
Haman's daughter empties the chamber pot onto Haman as he leads Mordecai in a royal procession. (Leipzig Universitätsbibliothek [University Library, ms. v. 1102], Leipzig, Germany)

Printed in the United States of America

718-221-6900
WWW.MYJLI.COM

Outsmarting Antisemitism

On the absurdity of antisemitism
and how to beat it with purpose,
positivity and pride

STUDENT TEXTBOOK

ADVISORY BOARD *of* GOVERNORS

Yaakov and Karen Cohen
Potomac, MD

Yitzchok and Julie Gniwisch
Montreal, QC

Barbara Hines
Aspen, CO

Ellen Marks
S. Diego, CA

David Mintz, OBM
Tenafly, NJ

Dr. Stephen F. Serbin
Columbia, SC

Leonard A. Wien, Jr.
Miami Beach, FL

PARTNERING FOUNDATIONS

Avi Chai Foundation

The David Samuel Rock Foundation

The Diamond Foundation

Estate of Elliot James Belkin

Francine Gani Charitable Fund

Goldstein Family Foundation

Kohelet Foundation

Kosins Family Foundation

Mayberg Foundation

Meromim Foundation

Myra Reinhard Family Foundation

The Robbins Family Foundation

Ruderman Family Foundation

William Davidson Foundation

World Zionist Organization

Yehuda and Anne Neuberger
Philanthropic Fund

The Zalik Foundation

PRINCIPAL BENEFACTOR

George Rohr
New York, NY

PILLARS *of* JEWISH LITERACY

Shaya Boymelgreen
Miami Beach, FL

Pablo and Sara Briman
Mexico City, Mexico

Zalman and Mimi Fellig
Miami Beach, FL

Yosef and Chana Malka Gorowitz
Redondo Beach, CA

Shloimy and Mirele Greenwald
Brooklyn, NY

Dr. Vera Koch Groszmann
S. Paulo, Brazil

Carolyn Hessel
New York, NY

Howard Jonas
Newark, New Jersey

David and Debra Magerman
Gladwyne, PA

Yitzchak Mirilashvili
Herzliya, Israel

Ben Nash
New Jersey

Eyal and Aviva Postelnik
Marietta, GA

Lee and Patti Schear
Dayton, OH

Isadore and Roberta Schoen
Fairfax, VA

Yair Shamir
Savyon, Israel

Larry Sifen
Virginia Beach, VA

SPONSORS

Mark and Rebecca Bolinsky
Long Beach, NY

Daniel and Eta Cotlar
Houston, TX

Rabbi Meyer and Leah Eichler
Brooklyn, NY

Steve and Esther Feder
Los Angeles, CA

Yoel Gabay
Brooklyn, NY

Brian and Dana Gavin
Houston, TX

Shmuel and Sharone Goodman
Chicago, IL

Adam and Elisheva Hendry
Miami, FL

Michael and Andrea Leven
Atlanta, GA

Joe and Shira Lipsey
Aspen, CO

Josef Michelashvili
Glendale, NY

Harvey Miller
Chicago, IL

Rachelle Nedow
El Paso, TX

Peter and Hazel Pflaum
Newport Beach, CA

Abe Podolak
Princeton Junction, NJ

Dr. Ze'ev Rav-Noy
Los Angeles, CA

Clive and Zoe Rock
Irvine, CA

Zvi Ryzman
Los Angeles, CA

Alan Zekelman
Bloomfield Hills, MI

Myrna Zisman
Cedarhurst, NY

Janice and Ivan Zuckerman
Coral Gables, FL

The Rohr Jewish Learning Institute
gratefully acknowledges the pioneering
and ongoing support of

George and Pamela Rohr

Since its inception, the Rohr JLI has been
a beneficiary of the vision, generosity, care,
and concern of the Rohr family.

In the merit of the tens of thousands of hours
of Torah study by JLI students worldwide,
may they be blessed with health, *Yiddishe
nachas* from all their loved ones, and
extraordinary success in all their endeavors.

DEDICATED TO

Lee and Patti Schear

Dayton, Ohio

JLI is indebted and deeply grateful for
their partnership in bringing Torah study
to all corners of the world and honors
their exemplary commitment to Jewish
literacy, Am Yisrael, and Eretz Yisrael.

In the merit of the Torah study by
thousands of students worldwide,
may they be blessed with good health,
happiness, *nachat* from their loved ones,
and success in all their endeavors.

Citation Types

SCRIPTURE

Biblical works were initially composed as handcrafted scrolls. Printed versions later became advantageous for study purposes, but a handcrafted scroll is used for the ritual synagogue reading of the Pentateuch, preserving the authenticity and sacredness of our ancient heritage.

SCRIPTURAL COMMENTARY

Throughout the ages, Jews scrutinized the Torah's text, generating many commentaries.

TALMUD AND MIDRASH

The Talmud and Midrash record the teachings of the sages—fundamental links in the unbroken chain of the Torah's transmission going back to Mount Sinai.

TALMUDIC COMMENTARY

The layers of Talmudic teaching have been rigorously excavated in each era, resulting in a library of insightful commentaries.

JEWISH MYSTICISM

The mystics explore the inner, esoteric depths. The icon for mystical texts reflects the "*sefirot* tree" commonly present in kabbalistic charts.

JEWISH PHILOSOPHY

Jewish philosophic texts shed light on all of life's big questions. They often demonstrate the relevance of Jewish teachings even as the sands of societal values continuously shift.

JEWISH LAW AND CUSTOM

The guidance that emerges from Scripture and the Talmud finds practical expression in Jewish law, known as *halachah* ("the way"), alongside customs adopted by Jewish communities through the generations.

CHASIDUT

Chasidism's advent in the eighteenth century brought major, encouraging changes to Jewish life and outlook. Its teachings are akin to refreshing, life-sustaining waters from a continuously flowing well of the profoundest insights.

PERSPECTIVES

Personal, professional, and academic perspectives, expressed in essays, research papers, diaries, and other works, can often enhance appreciation for Torah ideas and the totality of the Jewish experience.

Contents

Foreword

"THE WOLF WILL DWELL BESIDE THE LAMB;
A LEOPARD WILL RELAX ALONGSIDE A KID GOAT."

— ISAIAH 11:6

Maimonides interprets Isaiah's prophecy of coexisting creatures as foretelling the extinction of antisemitism: Jews existed for millennia as a lone lamb cornered by hostile forces, but eventually, peoples formerly bent on annihilation or harm will live harmoniously with us.

Despite impressive strides in tolerance and equality, Isaiah's vision of coexistence remains somewhat otherworldly. Recent surveys of American Jews demonstrate that antisemitism is a clear and dominant concern. A survey of British Jews found that 42 percent have considered leaving the U.K., and 85 percent of those cited antisemitism in politics as their motivation. Antisemitism remains a global hot topic in news, politics, and social media, and at schools and college campuses.

Amid a world of confusion and occasional despair, The Rohr Jewish Learning Institute saw the need for a systematic course on the topic. We have therefore produced *Outsmarting Antisemitism*, a revolutionary four-week public offering geared to help participants beat antisemitism with purpose, positivity, and pride. The course—suitable for the individual and the policy maker, for the leader and layperson alike—enlists historical analysis, Talmudic sources, Jewish mysticism, and contemporary expert analysis to provide insight, perspective, practical direction, and personal reassurance.

Outsmarting Antisemitism examines the roots of this ancient hatred and probes productive strategies for reducing antisemitism, best practices for dealing with prejudiced public individuals, tools for coping with personal fears triggered by antisemitism, and the role of faith in these areas. The course investigates the modern fire-breathing dragon—anti-Israel-focused antisemitism—and highlights methods of forestalling Jewish youth from unwittingly lending their voices to antisemitic agendas. The learning experience will be informative, empowering, and, at the same time, motivational and supportive.

It is our fervent hope that these currently indispensable methods of coping and handling become rapidly obsolete. We pray that this course will soon be reshelved in the history department, rather than persist as a contemporary social instrument—with the speedy realization of Isaiah's vision of global harmony, mutual understanding, and genuine goodwill.

Endorsements

"What distinguishes the present moment is the rise of Antisemitism simultaneously on all the fronts—New Antisemitism on the left, Classic Antisemitism on the right, and Antisemitism of Islamic extremists. To succeed in the struggle against these dangerous phenomena, we have to confront Antisemitism on all fronts simultaneously.

Therefore, this course from the Rohr Jewish Learning Institute is very important. I applaud their efforts."

NATAN SHARANSKY

Chairman, Institute for the Study of Global Antisemitism and Policy (ISGAP)

Author, *Defending Identity: Its Indispensable Role in Protecting Democracy,* and other titles

---

"*Outsmarting Antisemitism* could scarcely appear at a better moment. As hatred of Jews resurges across the world, Jews everywhere wrestle with the question of what causes it and how best to respond. This volume supplies time-tested answers."

JONATHAN D. SARNA, PHD

Joseph H. and Belle R. Braun Professor of American Jewish History

Brandeis University

Author, *When General Grant Expelled the Jews,* and many other titles

---

"You don't have to agree with every assumption, question, or answer to recognize the uniqueness and importance of this book. Beyond the statistics of current antisemitism, it offers a historic and philosophical roadmap through history to understand the core nature of our people and faith, and urges us not to allow antisemites to define the narrative and destiny of the Jewish people."

RABBI ABRAHAM COOPER

Associate Dean and Director, Global Social Action
The Simon Wiesenthal Center

"If ever there were a time when a solid course was needed on understanding and combating resurgent antisemitism, now is such a time."

ALVIN H. ROSENFELD, PHD

Professor of English and Jewish Studies
Irving M. Glazer Chair in Jewish Studies
Indiana University
Director, Institute for the Study of Contemporary Antisemitism
Author of *Resurgent Antisemitism* and *Deciphering the New Antisemitism*, and other titles

---

"All those who care about religious freedom, both Jews and others, confront a disturbing increase in antisemitism worldwide. It is no longer enough just to be opposed to antisemitism. We all have to be knowledgeable about its history and current manifestations if we are to be equipped to combat its spread. That is why this course matters."

CARY NELSON, PHD

Professor Emeritus
University of Illinois at Urbana-Champaign
Past President, American Association of University Professors

"For the past two generations, only a small fraction of the global Jewish community has experienced antisemitism first-hand, leading many to question whether the hatred that has been described as the world's oldest is becoming a relic of the past, or if we have merely been living through the benign phase of a cycle that remains constant. Recent incidents in Europe and North America make this question increasingly relevant and pressing. This course comes at a particularly opportune moment in history."

TAL KEINAN

Author, *G-d Is in the Crowd: Twenty-First-Century Judaism*

"Although almost 150 years have passed since Leo Pinsker sounded the alarm over the psychological illness and politically monstrous evil of antisemitism, each generation of Jews must guard themselves against it. The hard and sad truth is that antisemitism has not and evidently will not disappear. The first step for Jews today in confronting antisemitism is to understand what it is by developing and cultivating Jewish education."

STEPHEN GROSBY, PHD

Professor of Religion Emeritus
Clemson University

Author, *Hebraism in Religion, History, and Politics: The Third Culture*

"Antisemitism is back in the open. Not only in the Mideast or in Europe, but also in North America and even right here in the United States. We're blessed in Ohio—as are many communities across the country—with a bipartisan list of elected officials, clergy, and civic leaders ready to take on what's been called the world's oldest hatred. But in order to defeat it, we must first understand it. This JLI course can provide necessary context for community leaders and public policymakers alike to know how to speak out and when to take action against resurgent hatred of the Jewish people."

HOWIE BEIGELMAN

Executive Director, Ohio Jewish Communities

"Antisemitism is an ancient hatred that has taken many forms over the centuries and led to the autos de fé, forced assimilation, ethnic cleansing and genocide. Today, we have a "new" variant of antisemitism in the form of anti-Israel activism. This course tackles the age-old issue of antisemitism by looking at the remarkable endurance of the Jews. It looks directly at the source of antisemitism and delineates how the source of this hatred is not the Jews but how others perceive the Jews. Further, it examines how this perception of Jews has morphed with the advent of the vibrant Jewish State of Israel over the past seventy-three years. Now we have anti-Israel activism as a cover for antisemitism. Finally, it discusses the impact of behavioral psychology and neuroscience on the minds of those who embrace the scourge of antisemitism. As we see from the course, one type of antisemitism metastasizes to another, but it is all antisemitism, and young Jews as well as all Jews must learn how to confront it with candor and poise as well as trust that antisemitism will one day be obsolete and we will realize and enjoy Isaiah's vision of the harmony in the world as the leopard and kid goat lie down alongside each other in peace."

CAROLE BASRI, ESQ.

Visiting Professor, Peking University School of Transactional Law
Producer, *The Last Jews of Baghdad: End of an Exile, Beginning of a Journey*

Accreditation

FOR MEDICAL PRACTITIONERS

ACCREDITATION STATEMENT

This activity has been planned and implemented in accordance with the accreditation requirements and policies of the **Accreditation Council for Continuing Medical Education (ACCME)** through the joint providership of New York Medical College and the Rohr Jewish Learning Institute. New York Medical College is accredited by the ACCME to provide continuing medical education for physicians.

CREDITS DESIGNATION

New York Medical College designates this live activity for a maximum of ***9.0 AMA PRA Category I Credits™***. Physicians should claim only the credit commensurate with the extent of their participation in the activity.

AMERICAN DISABILITY ACT STATEMENT

New York Medical College fully complies with the legal requirements of the Americans with Disabilities Act. If you require special assistance, please submit your request in writing thirty (30) days in advance of the activity, to continuingeducation@myjli.com

CONFLICT OF INTEREST DISCLOSURE POLICY

The "**Conflict of Interest Disclosure Policy**" of New York Medical College requires that faculty participating in any CME activity disclose to the audience any relationship(s) with a pharmaceutical product or device company. Any presenter, whose disclosed relationships prove to create a conflict of interest with regard to their contribution to the activity, will not be permitted to present.

New York Medical College also requires that faculty participating in any CME activity disclose to the audience when discussing any unlabeled or investigational use of any commercial product or device not yet approved for use in the United States. New York Medical College and ACCME staff have no conflicts of interest with commercial interests related directly or indirectly to this educational activity.

DISCLOSURE OF COMMERCIAL SUPPORT AND THE UNLABELED USE OF A COMMERCIAL PRODUCT

No member of the planning committee and no member of the faculty for this event has a financial interest or other relationship with any commercial product.

The members of the Planning Committee are:

Edward I. Reichman, M.D.—Reviewer
Professor of Emergency Medicine and Epidemiology & Population Health, Albert Einstein College of Medicine

Disclosure: Dr. Reichman presents no relevant conflict of interest.

Mindy Wallach—Course Administrator
The Rohr Jewish Learning Institute

Disclosure: Mrs. Wallach presents no relevant conflict of interest.

To claim credit for attending the course (9 credits), professionals should request credit and submit their name, profession, email, and mailing address to their instructor or online at: **myJLI.com/continuingeducation** at the beginning of the course.

Instructions on how to complete course evaluations and download your certificate will follow by email.

Accreditation

FOR ATTORNEYS

The course

Outsmarting Antisemitism

has been approved in these states for fulfillment of the continuing education requirements for legal and ethics credits:

United States

Alabama
Alaska
Arkansas
California
Colorado
Connecticut
Delaware
Florida
Georgia
Idaho
Illinois
Indiana
Iowa
Kansas
Kentucky
Louisiana *
Minnesota *
Missouri
Nevada *
New Jersey
North Carolina
Ohio *
Oklahoma
Oregon *
Pennsylvania
Rhode Island
South Carolina
Tennessee
Utah
Washington
Wisconsin *

*Pending approval at the time this book went to print

LESSON 1

DETAIL FROM THE *BARCELONA HAGGADAH*
ca. 1340. (British Library, London)

THE ETERNAL PEOPLE

By taking another look at the statistics, studying our people's remarkable perseverance, and exploring the concept of Providence, we can find eternal cause for confidence and optimism while we implement plans to secure ourselves and our communities.

I. A CONCERNING RISE

Welcome to *Outsmarting Antisemitism,* an empowering new course from the Rohr Jewish Learning Institute on how to beat antisemitism with purpose, positivity, and pride.

The topic of this course is, unfortunately, quite relevant. Over the past two decades, a fresh surge of antisemitic incidents has been seen in numerous countries.

Antisemitic color etching by Thomas Rowlandson (1757–1827), an English artist and caricaturist, depicting an old peddler, with stereotypical Jewish features, being robbed by Gentile children. He looks up at coins that the children have tossed in the air, thus invoking the famous stereotype about Jews and money. Historically, art has played a significant role in the dissemination of antisemitism. (Katz Ehrenthal Collection, United States Holocaust Memorial Museum, Washington, D.C.)

Steven Spielberg talks about rising antisemitism: ***myjli.com/antisemitism***

FIGURE 1.1

Leaving the U.K.?

Antisemitism Barometer, 2019
(London: Campaign Against Antisemitism), p. 28

"In the past two years I have considered leaving Britain due to antisemitism."

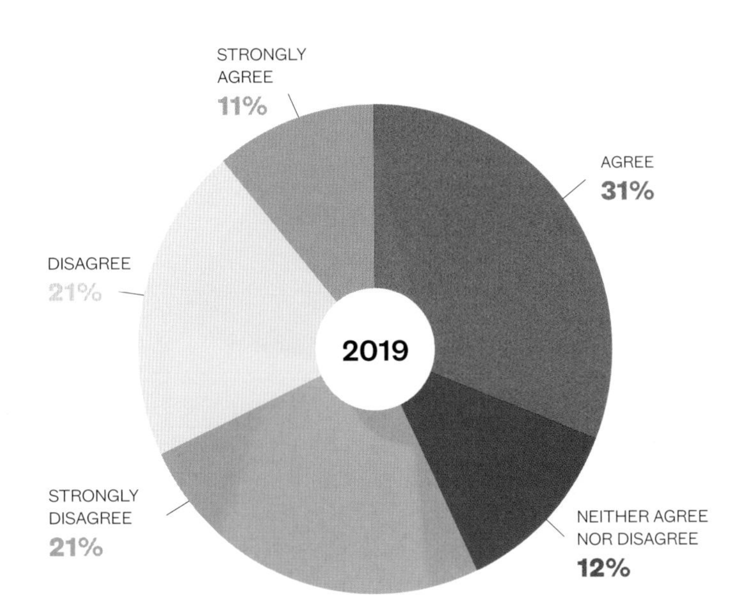

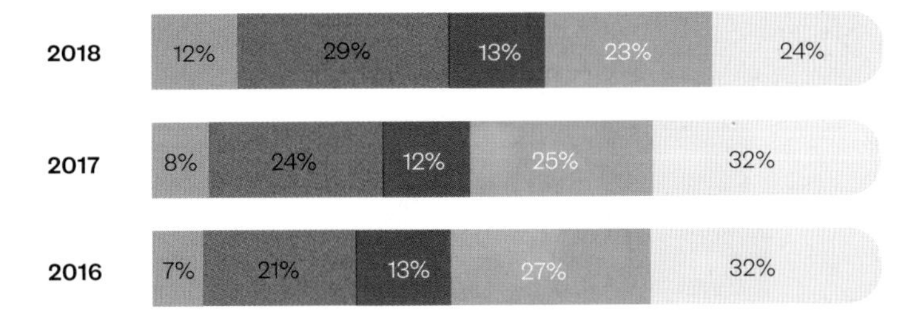

FIGURE 1.2

Public Displays of Judaism, U.K.

Antisemitism Barometer, 2019
(London: Campaign Against Antisemitism), p. 32

"Due to antisemitsm, I try not to show visible signs of my Judaism when I go out, like a Star of David or a Jewish skullcap (kippah)."

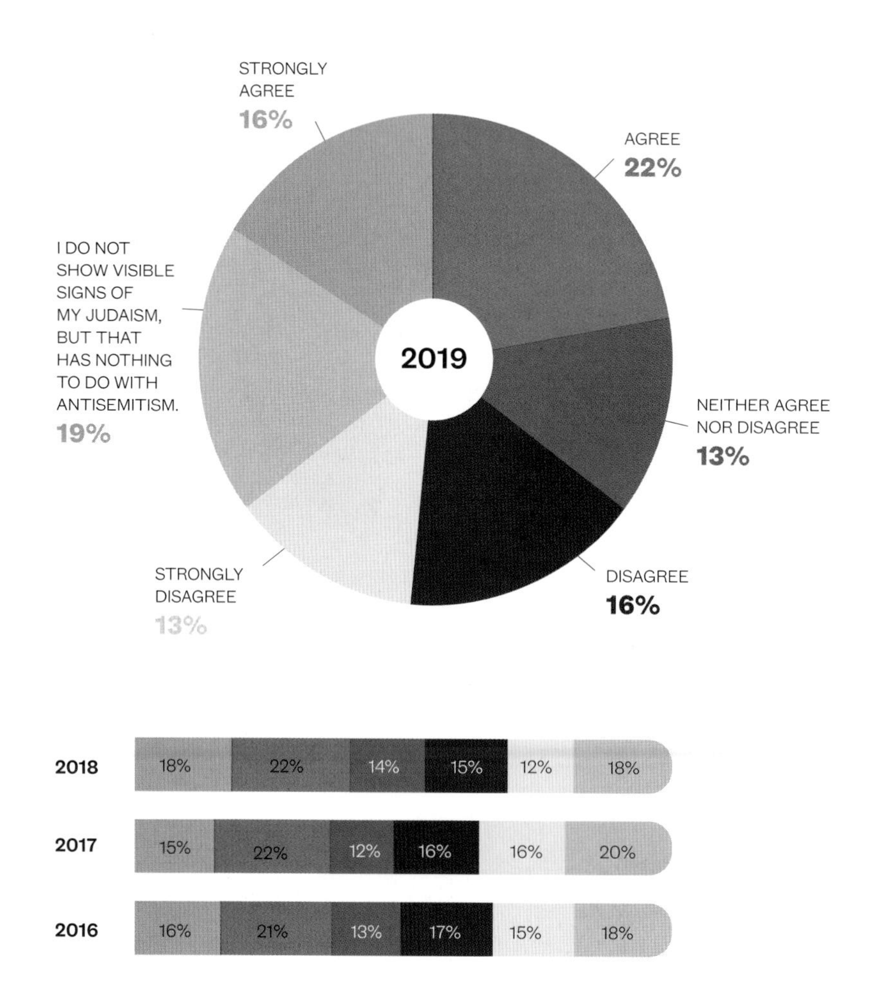

FIGURE 1.3

Antisemitic Incidents: United States, 2009–2019

"Audit of Antisemitic Incidents 2019," Major Findings (Anti-Defamation League)

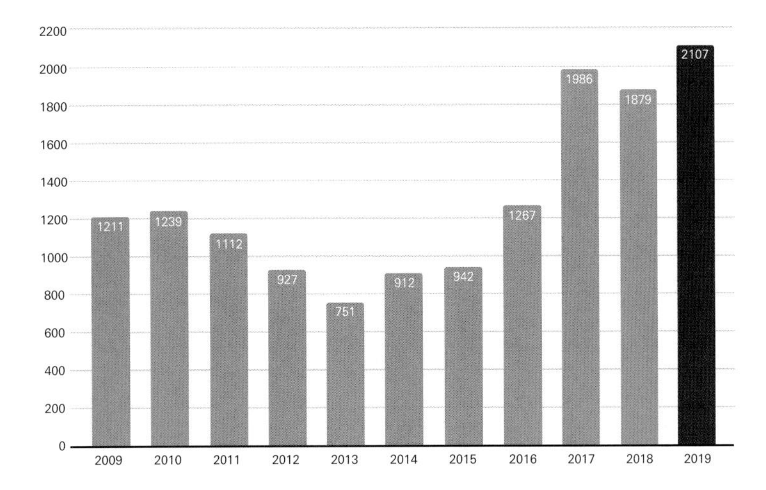

Under the Imperial Russian coat of arms, Russian Jews, packs in hand, line Europe's shore as they gaze across the ocean. Waiting for them under an American eagle holding a banner with the legend "Shelter me in the shadow of Your wings" (Psalms 17:8), are their American relatives, whose outstretched arms welcome them to their new home. (Hebrew Publishing Company, 1909)

FIGURE 1.4

Antisemitic Incidents in Australia

"Report on Antisemitism in Australia 2020"
(Executive Council of Australian Jewry), p. 23

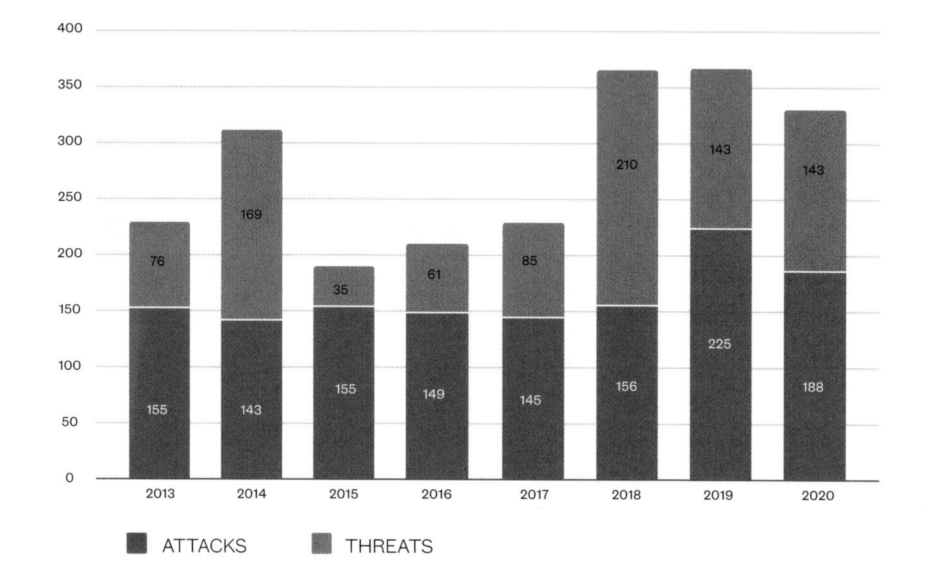

FIGURE 1.5

Antisemitic Incidents in Canada

"Annual Audit of Antisemitic Incidents, 2019"
(B'nai Brith of Canada), p. 12

INCIDENT TYPE	2014	2015	2016	2017	2018	2019
Harassment	1370	1123	1559	1409	1809	2011
Vandalism	238	136	158	327	221	182
Violence	19	10	11	16	11	14
TOTAL	1627	1269	1728	1752	2041	2207

II. COURSE MISSION

For many Jews, particularly in the twentieth century, responding or reacting to antisemitism has been a significant component of their Jewish identity.

It is certainly justified and commendable to recall our painful past and vigilantly tackle the antisemitism of today. At the same time, being Jewish should not be a mere response to—and in reaction to—antisemites.

This course will not lose sight of this larger truth, even while it addresses some highly pertinent questions about Jew-hatred that people are asking in today's climate.

Vellum scroll with an eyewitness account of a pogrom that occurred on April 6, 1918, in Novhorod-Siverskyi, Russia (now Ukraine). Written soon after the pogrom, it recounts the events, denounces the perpetrators, and records the names of the men, women, and children who were murdered. The last wave of pogroms in Russia took place in connection with the Revolution of 1917 and the chaos that accompanied the Ukrainian-Soviet War (1917–21). They far exceeded the earlier outbreaks in both size and severity. (Katz Ehrenthal Collection, United States Holocaust Memorial Museum, Washington, D.C.)

FIGURE 1.6

Essential to Being Jewish

Jewish Americans in 2020 (Pew Research Center), p. 64

What's essential to being Jewish?

% of U.S. Jews who say ______ is an essential part of what being Jewish means to them	
Remembering the Holocaust	76
Leading an ethical and moral life	72
Working for justice/equality	59
Being intellectually curious	56
Continuing family traditions	51
Caring about Israel	45
Having a good sense of humor	34
Being part of a Jewish community	33
Eating traditional Jewish foods	20
Observing Jewish law	15

TEXT 1A

Antisemitism Is Not the Sum Total

Deborah E. Lipstadt, *Antisemitism: Here and Now* (New York: Schocken, 2019), p. 240

Most Jews will immediately step forward when Jews anywhere are being attacked by antisemites. This is of course as it should be. What is regrettable, however, is that for some Jews, the fight against antisemitism becomes the sum total of their Jewish identity.

Recently, a much-respected Jewish communal leader lamented to me that he regretted not having educated his children about Jewish traditions and culture. He was, however, very proud of the fact that he had embedded within them a total intolerance of antisemitism. His kids were prepared to be at the barricades to do battle against this hatred, and many others as well.

His comments made me sad. Antisemitism has become the drummer to which his family's Jewish identity marches. They know of Jew as object, not subject. In other words, what is done *to* Jews becomes far more significant than what Jews *do*. This well-intentioned Jewish father has deprived his children of a rich and multifaceted legacy. They have been taught to see themselves mainly as perennial victims. This cedes to the oppressor control over one's destiny. It leaves many Jews, including this man's children, aware of what to be *against* but not what to be *for*.

DEBORAH E. LIPSTADT 1947–

Historian. Lipstadt is best known as author of the books *Denying the Holocaust, History on Trial, The Eichmann Trial,* and *Antisemitism: Here and Now*. She founded the Institute for Jewish Studies at Emory University, serving as its first director from 1998–2008. Lipstadt was a historical consultant to the United States Holocaust Memorial Museum and helped design the section of the museum dedicated to the American response to the Holocaust. She is currently the Dorot Professor of Modern Jewish History and Holocaust Studies at Emory.

TEXT 1B

On Earth For

Bari Weiss, speaking at the No Hate, No Fear Solidarity March, New York City, January 5, 2020

The Jewish people were not put on Earth to be anti-antisemites.

We were put on Earth to be Jews.

BARI WEISS
1984–

Opinion writer. Weiss was an op-ed and book review editor at *The Wall Street Journal* before joining *The New York Times* in 2017 as an op-ed staff editor and writer about culture and politics until she resigned in 2020. She has also served as a senior editor at *Tablet*, an online magazine of Jewish politics and culture. In 2019 she authored her first book, *How to Fight Anti-Semitism.*

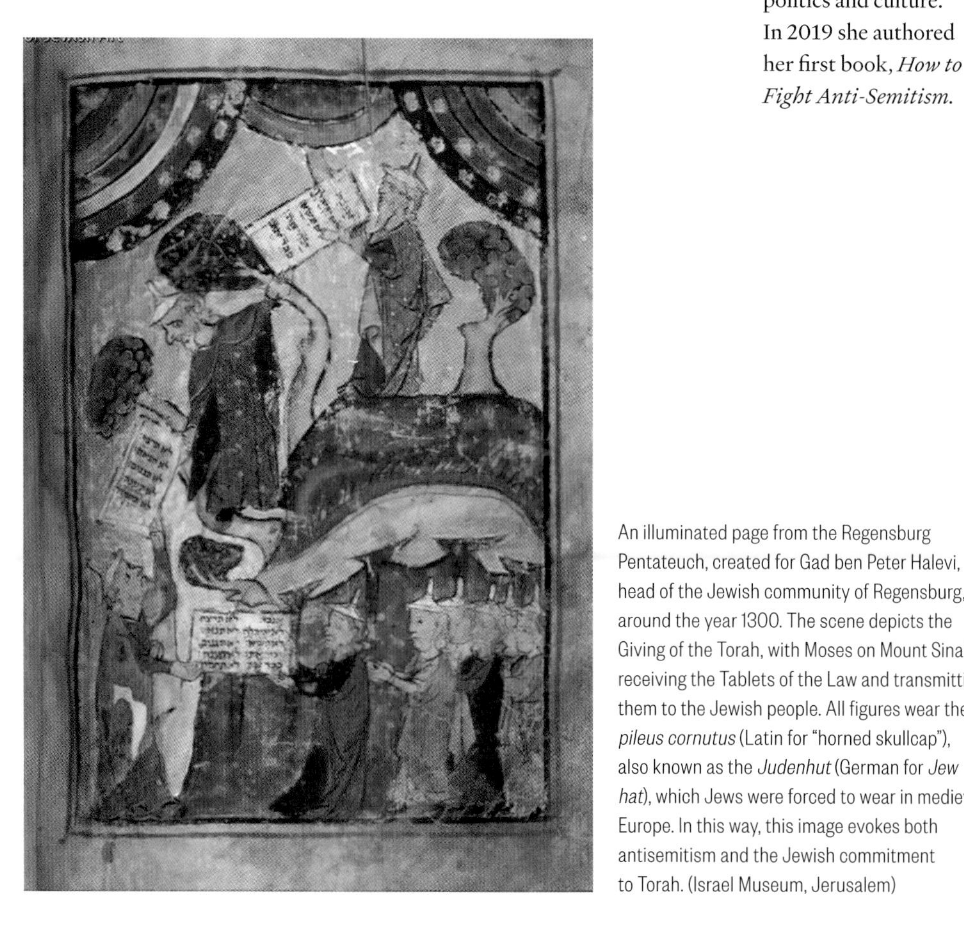

An illuminated page from the Regensburg Pentateuch, created for Gad ben Peter Halevi, head of the Jewish community of Regensburg, around the year 1300. The scene depicts the Giving of the Torah, with Moses on Mount Sinai receiving the Tablets of the Law and transmitting them to the Jewish people. All figures wear the *pileus cornutus* (Latin for "horned skullcap"), also known as the *Judenhut* (German for *Jew hat*), which Jews were forced to wear in medieval Europe. In this way, this image evokes both antisemitism and the Jewish commitment to Torah. (Israel Museum, Jerusalem)

Bari Weiss delivers a powerful speech protesting antisemitic attacks in New York City: ***myjli.com/antisemitism***

FIGURE 1.7

The Course's Driving Questions

1.	What are some tools for coping with fears triggered by antisemitism?
2.	What role does faith play in addressing antisemitism?
3.	What are the best strategies to reduce antisemitism?
4.	What are the root causes of antisemitism? How does identifying these factors impact our efforts to prevent the hatred?
5.	How can we counter Israel-focused antisemitism? And how can we determine when criticism of Israel is antisemitic?
6.	How can we forestall well-meaning Jewish youth from unwittingly lending their voices to antisemitic agendas?
7.	What's the best strategy for dealing with a public figure who takes an unfavorable position toward us?

III. THE ONLY THING TO FEAR

The first step in this course is to analyze the natural emotional and practical reactions to antisemitism:

EXERCISE 1.1

1. **Have you or anyone close to you recently been the victim of a verbal or physical antisemitic assault?**

   Yes **No**

   If no, consider a recent antisemitic incident that you heard about.

   Incident:

2. **What were your immediate feelings after the incident?**

   a

   b

3. **What were some actions that you or others around you took as a result of the incident?**

   a

   b

TEXT 2

Anxiety Drawbacks

Talmud, Sanhedrin 100b

דִּכְתִיב: לֹא תַּעֵיל דַּוְיָא בְּלִבָּךְ דְּגַבְרֵי גִּיבָּרִין קְטַל דַּוְיָא . . .

שְׁלֹמֹה אַמְרָהּ: דְּאָגָה בְלֶב אִישׁ יַשְׁחֶנָּה (מִשְׁלֵי יב, כה).

It is stated in the book of Ben Sira: "Do not allow anxiety into your heart, for anxiety has killed the mighty." . . .

King Solomon said the same: "If there is anxiety in your heart—quash it!" (PROVERBS 12:25).

BABYLONIAN TALMUD

A literary work of monumental proportions that draws upon the legal, spiritual, intellectual, ethical, and historical traditions of Judaism. The 37 tractates of the Babylonian Talmud contain the teachings of the Jewish sages from the period after the destruction of the 2nd Temple through the 5th century CE. It has served as the primary vehicle for the transmission of the Oral Law and the education of Jews over the centuries; it is the entry point for all subsequent legal, ethical, and theological Jewish scholarship.

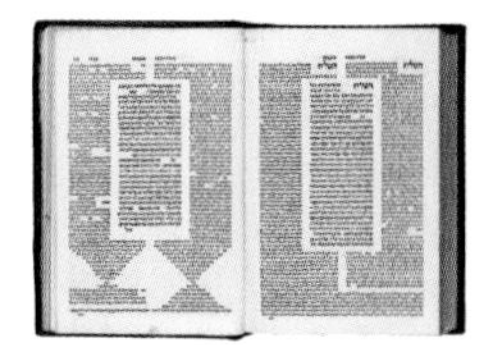

QUESTION

In the context of antisemitism, what might be some means of avoiding unhealthy panic?

IV. A MIRACULOUS PEOPLE

The call to reduce anxiety should not be misconstrued as an attempt to ignore reality and to bask in ignorance's bliss. Rather, it addresses a genuine need for the sake of channeling our concerns constructively.

One particularly effective method of accomplishing this is to reflect on the miracle of Jewish survival.

TEXT 3

Historical Anomaly

Deborah E. Lipstadt, Interviewed at the National Jewish Retreat, August 2019

The fact that we're here is such a historical anomaly, it makes no sense. So sometimes, when I'm asked about antisemitism, people will say, "Well, how can you be optimistic in all this? How can you see the positive? It's such a dreary situation!"

And I say, "Because we shouldn't be here. And the fact that we are here shouldn't be taken for granted."

Rabbi Yitzchak Breitowitz discusses the miracle of Jewish survival: ***myjli.com/antisemitism***

TEXT 4

Like Earth's Dust

Maimonides, *Epistle to Yemen*

וּכְבָר הִבְטִיחַ הַקָּדוֹשׁ בָּרוּךְ הוּא לְיַעֲקֹב אָבִינוּ עָלָיו הַשָּׁלוֹם,
שֶׁאַף עַל פִּי שֶׁיִּשְׁתַּעְבְּדוּ הָאוּמּוֹת בְּזַרְעוֹ וְיַעֲנוּ אוֹתָם
וְיִגְבְּרוּ עֲלֵיהֶם, הֵם יִישָּׁאֲרוּ וְיַעַמְדוּ, וְהַמִּשְׁתַּעַבְּדִים בָּהֶם
יַחְלְפוּ וְיֹאבֵדוּ. כְּמוֹ שֶׁנֶּאֱמַר "וְהָיָה זַרְעֲךָ כַּעֲפַר הָאָרֶץ"
(בְּרֵאשִׁית כח, יד). כְּלוֹמַר אַף עַל פִּי שֶׁהֵם נְתוּנִים לְמִרְמָס
וּלְמִרְפָּס כֶּעָפָר הַזֶּה שֶׁהַכֹּל דוֹרְסִים אוֹתוֹ - סוֹף שֶׁיִּגְבְּרוּ
וְיִנַּצֵּחוּ. וְכֵן עַל דֶּרֶךְ הַמָּשָׁל כְּמוֹ שֶׁהֶעָפָר בְּאַחֲרִיתוֹ יַעֲלֶה עַל
הַדּוֹרְסִים אוֹתוֹ וְיִישָּׁאֵר הוּא - וְהַדּוֹרְסִים אוֹתוֹ לֹא יַעֲמֹדוּ.
וְכֵן הִבְטִיחָנוּ הַבּוֹרֵא עַל יְדֵי נְבִיאָיו שֶׁלֹּא נֹאבַד וְלֹא יַעֲשֶׂה
עִמָּנוּ כְּלָיָה, וְלֹא נָסוּר לְעוֹלָם מִלִּהְיוֹת אוּמָּה חֲסִידָה. וּכְמוֹ
שֶׁאִי אֶפְשַׁר שֶׁיִּתְבַּטֵּל מְצִיאוּתוֹ שֶׁל הַקָּבָּ"ה, כֵּן אִי אֶפְשַׁר
שֶׁנֹּאבַד וְנִתְבַּטֵּל מִן הָעוֹלָם. שֶׁכֵּן אָמַר מַלְאָכִי, "אֲנִי ה'
לֹא שָׁנִיתִי וְאַתֶּם בְּנֵי יַעֲקֹב לֹא כְלִיתֶם" (מַלְאָכִי ג, ו).

G-d* assured our father Jacob early on that although the nations would enslave his descendants, treat them cruelly, and subjugate them, his children would survive and endure, whereas those who enslaved them would eventually disappear. G-d told him (GENESIS 28:14), "Your descendants will be like the dust of the earth." Although they are destined to be trampled and downtrodden

* Throughout this book, "G-d" and "L-rd" are written with a hyphen instead of an "o" (both in our own translations and when quoting others). This is one way we accord reverence to the sacred divine name. This also reminds us that, even as we seek G-d, He transcends any human effort to describe His reality.

RABBI MOSHE BEN MAIMON (MAIMONIDES, RAMBAM) 1135–1204

Halachist, philosopher, author, and physician. Maimonides was born in Córdoba, Spain. After the conquest of Córdoba by the Almohads, he fled Spain and eventually settled in Cairo, Egypt. There, he became the leader of the Jewish community and served as court physician to the vizier of Egypt. He is most noted for authoring the *Mishneh Torah*, an encyclopedic arrangement of Jewish law; and for his philosophical work, *Guide for the Perplexed*. His rulings on Jewish law are integral to the formation of halachic consensus.

as everyone tramples the dust of the earth, they will overcome and triumph in the end, just as, to continue the analogy, the dust eventually rises over those who trampled upon it [when their corpses are buried]. So Israel will remain in existence, whereas those who have trodden upon her will not. . . .

The Creator similarly assured us through His prophets that we will never be destroyed, that He will never permit our annihilation, and that we will never stray from being a nation devoted to its purpose. Just as it is impossible for G-d's own existence to be nullified, so is it impossible that we should be destroyed and eliminated from the world. So spoke Malachi (3:6): "I am G-d and I have not changed, and you, the Children of Jacob, have not been destroyed."

The *Golden Haggadah,* was copied and illuminated on vellum in Catalonia in approximately 1320 CE. The manuscript takes its name from the 56 miniature paintings at the beginning of the book that depict biblical scenes set against gold-tooled backgrounds. Presented here is the drawing of Jacob's dream, in which he was told, "Your descendants will be like the dust of the earth" (Genesis 28:14), interpreted by Maimonides as a promise about Jewish survival. (British Library [MS 27210], London)

V. CONSIDER THE FULL PICTURE

We are living in much better times for Jews than in previous generations. The vast majority of Jews do not live under antisemitic regimes. And while individual acts of antisemitism have risen, fewer people overall harbor antisemitic sentiments than previously. This knowledge should help reduce our panic.

Postcard published in Krakow, Poland, in 1888, depicting a class of boys walking with their teachers to a Simchat Torah celebration carrying decorated flags. The text at the bottom of the postcard reads, "*Gang zu Kufes*," meaning, "Going to the *Hakafot*." *Hakafot* is the tradition of marching around the synagogue in song and dance with the Torah scrolls, the highlight of the Simchat Torah holiday. (National Library of Israel, Jerusalem)

FIGURE 1.8

Stereotypes about Jews—Index Questions

"Antisemitic Attitudes in the U.S." (Anti-Defamation League, 2019)

" Jews stick together more than other Americans.

" Jews always like to be at the head of things.

" Jews are more loyal to Israel than to America.

" Jews have too much power in the business world.

" Jews have too much control and influence on Wall Street.

" Jews are just as honest as other business people. (Probably false.)

" Jews don't care what happens to anyone but their own kind.

" Jews have too much power in the United States today.

" Jewish businessmen are so shrewd that other people do not have a fair chance at competition.

" Jews are more willing than others to use shady practices to get what they want.

" Jews have a lot of irritating faults.

FIGURE 1.9

Stereotypes about Jews—Index Results

"Antisemitic Attitudes in the U.S." (Anti-Defamation League, 2019)

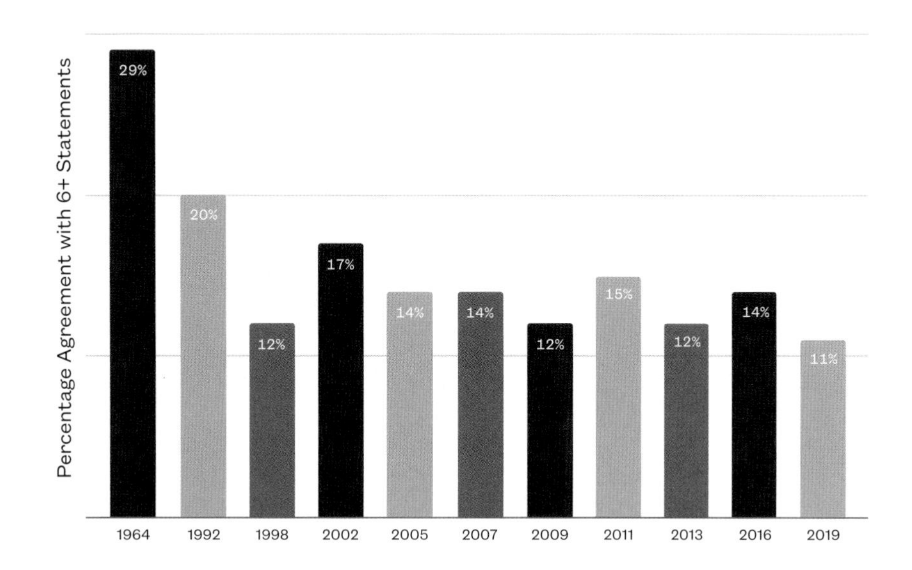

MOBILIZE ALL THE PEOPLE
JEWISH AND GENTILE
TO STOP ANTI-SEMITISM!

MASS MEETING - SYMPHONY HALL
SUNDAY, OCTOBER 24th, AT 8 P. M.

OTIS A. HOOD, candidate for School Committee, was the first person in Boston to rip the cover off the anti-Semitic attacks spreading in Dorchester and Roxbury. He continues to do this in his broadcasts on Sundays over Station WNAC at 1:15 P. M.

Now the campaign has been picked up by the newspaper PM published in New York. It is good for the facts to be known to all, so that the progressive forces of the people can be mobilized against the 5th columnists responsible.

BUT THE NEWSPAPER PM HAS TRIED TO TURN THE WHOLE THING INTO AN ATTACK AGAINST GOVERNOR SALTONSTALL.

While the Governor could have displayed more energy in taking action on previous indications of this menace, the main responsibility cannot be justly placed at his door and a political football made of this issue.

WHAT HAS TO BE DONE?

The whole people of Boston should unite to guarantee that the Christian Front, which instigates these attacks, is cleaned out.

The schools should undertake a vigorous campaign to explain to all the children that anti-Semitism is Hitler's weapon against America. The churches — Catholic, Jewish, and Protestant — should undertake a campaign to enlighten their congregations and mobilize them to fight anti-Semitism.

The public authorities should take systematic action to arrest and prosecute the instigators of this propaganda. We feel sure these will be found among the vicious enemies of President Roosevelt, of the Soviet Union, of the war effort.

The AFL and CIO unions should undertake a campaign of education in every war plant and factory.

Hear Otis A. Hood, candidate for Boston School Committee, speak at the tremendous mass meeting in Symphony Hall Sunday, October 24, at 8 P. M.

TUNE IN ON STATION WNAC EVERY SUNDAY AT 1:15 P. M.
TO HEAR HIM SPEAK ON THIS ISSUE

ISSUED BY: COMMUNIST PARTY OF BOSTON, 15 ESSEX STREET, BOSTON 11

Handbill from October 1940 announcing a mass meeting in Boston to stop antisemitism. The meeting was a response to anti-Jewish attacks in Dorchester and Roxbury by the Christian Front, an antisemitic, pro-Nazi organization, formed in 1938. The featured speaker, Otis Hood (d. 1983), chair of the Massachusetts Communist Party and frequent gubernatorial candidate, wanted to introduce education about antisemitism into the school curriculum. (Katz Ehrenthal Collection, United States Holocaust Memorial Museum, Washington, D.C.)

TEXT 5

Attitudes toward Jews

"ADL Poll: Anti-Semitic Attitudes in America Decline 3 Percent," adl.org, October 28, 2013

"It is heartening that attitudes toward Jews have improved over the last few years and, historically, have declined significantly in America," said Abraham H. Foxman, ADL National Director. "On the occasion of our centennial it causes us to take a broader perspective, to appreciate how far we have come in 100 years. In 1913 there were no surveys like this, but anti-Semitism was rife in public and private expressions, in universities, jobs and neighborhoods. In 1964, when we did our first survey, we found that 29 percent of Americans held anti-Semitic views. So we—and America—have made real progress."

World War I-era poster showing immigrants arriving in New York Harbor. The Yiddish caption reads, "Food will win the war! You came here seeking freedom, now you must help to preserve it. Wheat is needed for the allies. Waste nothing." It is signed by the United States Food Administration, a federal agency that controlled the production, distribution, and conservation of food in the U.S. during World War I. (Library of Congress, Washington, D.C.)

VI. I FEAR NOT, BECAUSE YOU ARE WITH ME

An important method that Jews have historically adopted to remain positive and avoid debilitating fear is to develop a trusting relationship with G-d.

TEXT 6

Fear No Evil

Psalms 23:1–2, 4

מִזְמוֹר לְדָוִד ה' רֹעִי לֹא אֶחְסָר. בִּנְאוֹת דֶּשֶׁא יַרְבִּיצֵנִי עַל מֵי מְנֻחוֹת יְנַהֲלֵנִי . . . גַּם כִּי אֵלֵךְ בְּגֵיא צַלְמָוֶת לֹא אִירָא רָע כִּי אַתָּה עִמָּדִי שִׁבְטְךָ וּמִשְׁעַנְתֶּךָ הֵמָּה יְנַחֲמֻנִי . . .

A song of David: G-d is my shepherd; I shall not lack. He allows me to lay down in green pastures; He leads me beside still waters. . . . Even if I walk in the valley of death's shadow, I will fear no evil—for You are with me. Your rod and Your staff—they comfort me. . . .

PSALMS

Biblical book. The book of Psalms contains 150 psalms expressing praise for G-d, faith in G-d, and laments over tragedies. The primary author of the psalms was King David, who lived in the 9th century BCE. Psalms also contains material from earlier figures. The feelings and circumstances expressed in the psalms resonate throughout the generations and they have become an important part of communal and personal prayer.

This is the oldest extant manuscript of Psalm 23, dated to the first century CE. Parts of this Psalms scroll were discovered at Nahal Hever in 1952, and additional fragments were excavated in 1960–61. The site is also known as the "Cave of Letters," due to letters of the second-century Jewish general, Bar Kochba, that were discovered there. The cave was used as refuge from Roman persecution during the second century. One can imagine that its inhabitants took solace when reading the words on this fragment, "Even if I walk in the valley of death's shadow, I will fear no evil—for You are with me." (The Leon Levy Dead Sea Scrolls Digital Library; Israel Antiquities Authority, Jerusalem [5/6Hev 1b 891 - 5/6Hev Ps], photo: Shai Halevi)

Is there a difference between psychological optimism and Jewish optimism? **Rabbi Mendel Kalmenson** explores: ***myjli.com/antisemitism***

TEXT 7

Confidence

Havdalah, opening verse (from Isaiah 12:2)

הִנֵּה אֵ-ל יְשׁוּעָתִי אֶבְטַח וְלֹא אֶפְחָד,
כִּי עָזִּי וְזִמְרָת יָ-הּ ה', וַיְהִי לִי לִישׁוּעָה.

Indeed, G-d is my deliverance. I am confident and I shall not fear. For G-d is my strength and my praise, and He has been my salvation.

ISAIAH

Biblical book. The book of Isaiah contains the prophecies of Isaiah, who lived in the 7–6th centuries BCE. Isaiah's prophecies contain stern rebukes for the personal failings of the contemporary people of Judea and the corruption of its government, as well as consolation and visions of the future Redemption.

The *Barcelona Haggadah*, was copied and illuminated on parchment in Catalonia in approximately 1340 CE. Its folios abound in illustrations depicting Passover rituals, biblical and Midrashic episodes, and symbolic foods. Many of these illustrations are presented in historiated initial-word panels, like the one presented here: an elderly man lifts a goblet while performing the *Havdalah* blessing alongside a young child holding the twisted candle that is traditionally used in this ceremony. (British Library [MS 14761], London)

TEXT 8

Never Alone

Sifrei, Behaalotecha 84

כָּל זְמַן שֶׁיִּשְׂרָאֵל מְשׁוּעְבָּדִים, כִּבְיָכוֹל שְׁכִינָה מִשְׁתַּעְבֶּדֶת עִמָּהֶם, שֶׁנֶּאֱמַר . . . "בְּכָל צָרָתָם לוֹ צָר" (יְשַׁעְיָה סג, ט).

Whenever Jews are persecuted, the G-dly presence is, so to speak, persecuted along with them. As it is stated . . . "In all of their pain, He is pained" (ISAIAH 63:9).

SIFREI

An early rabbinic Midrash on the biblical books of Numbers and Deuteronomy. *Sifrei* focuses mostly on matters of law, as opposed to narratives and moral principles. According to Maimonides, this halachic Midrash was authored by Rav, a 3rd-century Babylonian Talmudic sage.

TEXT 9

Cause and Effect

Psalms 32:10

וְהַבּוֹטֵחַ בַּה' חֶסֶד יְסוֹבְבֶנּוּ.

Those who trust in G-d will be surrounded by benevolence.

VII. TAKING ACTION

Having addressed emotions and mindsets, we must now focus on our actions:

The concept of trust in G-d inevitably creates the following challenge: What is the relationship between the practical steps we consider necessary to protect ourselves, and our powerful faith in G-d? An adage commonly cast into this discussion is that "G-d helps those who help themselves." But what exactly does that mean? And how does it work?

EXERCISE 1.2

Using the words "G-d" and "human action," craft a sentence that best expresses your impression of Judaism's vision for the divine-mortal interplay on matters like security.

TEXT 10

Esther's Plan

Esther 4:15–5:1

וַתֹּאמֶר אֶסְתֵּר לְהָשִׁיב אֶל מָרְדֳּכָי.

לֵךְ כְּנוֹס אֶת כָּל הַיְּהוּדִים הַנִּמְצְאִים בְּשׁוּשָׁן, וְצוּמוּ עָלַי וְאַל תֹּאכְלוּ וְאַל תִּשְׁתּוּ שְׁלֹשֶׁת יָמִים לַיְלָה וָיוֹם, גַּם אֲנִי וְנַעֲרֹתַי אָצוּם כֵּן, וּבְכֵן אָבוֹא אֶל־הַמֶּלֶךְ אֲשֶׁר לֹא כַדָּת וְכַאֲשֶׁר אָבַדְתִּי אָבָדְתִּי.

וַיַּעֲבֹר מָרְדֳּכָי, וַיַּעַשׂ כְּכֹל אֲשֶׁר צִוְּתָה עָלָיו אֶסְתֵּר.

וַיְהִי בַּיּוֹם הַשְּׁלִישִׁי וַתִּלְבַּשׁ אֶסְתֵּר מַלְכוּת, וַתַּעֲמֹד בַּחֲצַר בֵּית הַמֶּלֶךְ הַפְּנִימִית . . .

Esther dictated a message to be sent back to Mordecai:

"Go and assemble all the Jews who live in Shushan. Let them fast on my behalf. Let them neither eat nor drink for three days—night and day. I and my maidens will fast likewise. And then I shall go to the king, although it is contrary to the law. And if I am to perish, I shall perish."

BOOK OF ESTHER

The biblical account of the Purim story. By special request of Esther to the "Men of the Great Assembly," this book was included in the biblical canon. The Book of Esther is read from a scroll twice on the holiday of Purim, the holiday that commemorates the Jews' victory over their antisemitic enemies.

Mordecai went ahead and implemented
all that Esther had commanded him.

On the third day, Esther donned her royal apparel
and stood in the inner court of the king's palace. . . .

The North French Hebrew Miscellany is more a library than a book. Produced on parchment during the last quarter of the 13th century, it consists of eighty-four different groups of Judaic texts, with many of its 1,494 pages decorated with fine art. This page presents the Book of Ezra and Psalms, along with a miniature of Ahasuerus handing the golden scepter to Esther upon her unannounced visit in the king's inner court after days in fasting. (British Museum [MS 11639], London)

TEXT 11

Creating Space for G-d to Hide

Rabbi Menachem Mendel of Lubavitch,
Derech Mitzvotecha 107a

הַשֶּׁפַע בָּעוֹלָם הַזֶּה נִמְשֶׁכֶת דֶּרֶךְ לְבוּשׁ הַטֶּבַע, פֵּירוּשׁ שֶׁהִיא מִתְלַבֶּשֶׁת וּמִתְעַלֶּמֶת וּמִסְתַּתֶּרֶת עַד שֶׁנִּרְאֶה כְּאִילוּ עוֹלָם בְּמִנְהָגוֹ נוֹהֵג דֶּרֶךְ הַטֶּבַע. וּבֶאֱמֶת הַכֹּל בָּא מֵהַשֵּׁם יִתְבָּרֵךְ בִּכְבוֹדוֹ וּבְעַצְמוֹ, אֶלָּא שֶׁהוּא מַסְתִּיר שֶׁפַע אֱלֹקוּתוֹ כָּל כַּךְ עַד שֶׁלֹּא יֵרָאֶה בְּגִילוּי דְּבַר נִיסִיי וְיוֹצֵא מִנָּהוּג הָעוֹלָם, כִּי אִם שֶׁיֵּרָאֶה הַכֹּל כְּאִילוּ הוּא דָּבָר טִבְעִי.

לְמָשָׁל: כְּשֶׁנּוֹתֵן פַּרְנָסָה לְאִישׁ הַיִּשְׂרְאֵלִי דֵּי סִיפּוּקוֹ, אֵינוֹ נוֹתֵן לוֹ עַל יְדֵי נֵס, כְּמוֹ שֶׁיּוֹרִיד לוֹ מִן הַשָּׁמַיִם לֶחֶם וּבָשָׂר כְּמוֹ לְאוֹכְלֵי הַמָּן, שֶׁזֶּהוּ דָּבָר בִּלְתִּי טִבְעִי, אֶלָּא הוּא שׁוֹלֵחַ בִּרְכָתוֹ שֶׁיַּרְוִיחַ זֶה בְּמַשָּׂא וּמַתָּן בְּעֵסֶק. וְהִנֵּה הָרֶיוַח שֶׁעַל יְדֵי מַשָּׂא וּמַתָּן הוּא דָּבָר טִבְעִי, רָצָה לוֹמַר, שֶׁיָּכוֹל הָאוֹמֵר לוֹמַר "כֹּחִי וְעֹצֶם יָדִי עָשָׂה לִי אֶת כָּל הַחַיִל הַזֶּה" (דְּבָרִים ח, יז), וְ"חָכְמָתִי עָמְדָה לִּי" (קֹהֶלֶת ב, ט), שֶׁיָּדַעְתִּי בְּטוּב הַמִּסְחוֹר מַה לִּקְנוֹת וְאֵימָתַי לִמְכּוֹר, וּכְהַאי גַּוְונָא . . .

וְהוּא שֶׁיָּכִין לְבוּשׁ שֶׁבּוֹ וְעַל יָדוֹ יוּמְשַׁךְ הַשֶּׁפַע מִלְמַעְלָה בַּעֲשִׂיָּה. וְהַיְינוּ כְּשֶׁיִּהְיֶה לוֹ עֵסֶק נָכוֹן שֶׁלְּפִי טֶבַע הָעוֹלָם יְכוֹלִים לְהַרְוִיחַ סַךְ הַנִּצְרָךְ לוֹ בְּעֵסֶק זֶה, הֲרֵי זֶה לְבוּשׁ טוֹב שֶׁבּוֹ יַעֲלִים ה' בִּרְכָתוֹ . . . שֶׁהֲרֵי יְכוֹלִים לוֹמַר כֹּחִי וְעוֹצֶם יָדִי עָשָׂה לִי אֶת הַחַיִל הַזֶּה, מֵאַחַר שֶׁטִּבְעִיּוּת הָעוֹלָם לְהַרְוִיחַ כַּךְ. וּמִכֵּיוָן שֶׁיְּכוֹלִים לוֹמַר כַּךְ, הֲרֵי זֶה לְבוּשׁ נָכוֹן לְחֶסֶד זֶה . . .

בְּעָסְקוֹ בְּמַשָּׂא וּמַתָּן יְכַוֵּין שֶׁמַּאֲמִין שֶׁהַשֶּׁפַע בִּרְכַּת ה' הִיא כִּשְׁאָרֵי הַנִּסִּים הַגְּלוּיִם, כְּמוֹ

RABBI MENACHEM MENDEL OF LUBAVITCH *(TSEMACH TSEDEK)* 1789–1866

Chasidic rebbe and noted author. The *Tsemach Tsedek* was the third leader of the Chabad Chasidic movement and a noted authority on Jewish law. His numerous works include halachic responsa, Chasidic discourses, and kabbalistic writings. Active in the communal affairs of Russian Jewry, he worked to alleviate the plight of the cantonists, Jewish children kidnapped to serve in the Czar's army. He passed away in Lubavitch, leaving seven sons and two daughters.

שֶׁהוֹרִיד הַמָּן וְכַיּוֹצֵא, אֶלָּא שֶׁהוּא עוֹשֶׂה לְבוּשׁ לוֹ
יִתְבָּרֵךְ לְהַעֲלִים בִּרְכָתוֹ עַל יְדֵי עֵסֶק זֶה . . .

וּמִזֶּה יִלְמַד הָאָדָם בִּשְׁאָר עִסְקֵי הָעוֹלָם וּבְעִנְיָנָיו לִנְהוֹג
עַל דֶּרֶךְ זֶה . . . וְיַעֲשֶׂה הָעִנְיָן הַמִּצְטָרֵךְ לְפִי דַעְתּוֹ,
שֶׁיִּהְיֶה לְבוּשׁ שֶׁבְּאֶמְצָעִיתוֹ יִשְׁלַח ה' הַדָּבָר הַהוּא, וַה'
יַעֲשֶׂה הַטּוֹב בְּעֵינָיו, שֶׁהוּא הַטּוֹב הָאֲמִיתִּי הֲנָאוֹת לוֹ.

Everything that comes into being in this material world must materialize through natural means. Nature, however, is simply a garment, meaning, G-d's energy bringing things into existence must be dressed, concealed, and obscured to the point that an observer sees only a world that appears to run naturally. In truth, however, everything emerges directly from G-d Himself. He obscures the divine bestowals, until the miraculous and supernatural reality of material existence is not observable and material developments seem perfectly natural.

When, for example, G-d provides an individual with an ample livelihood, it is not done through a miracle as it was in the Sinai Desert, when G-d rained manna and meat from the skies. Rather, G-d sends the blessing through the individual's business affairs. The gains reaped through commerce appear so natural that the individual can be fooled into thinking along the lines of: "'It is *my* strength that generated this wealth'

(DEUTERONOMY 8:17), and, 'It is *my* wisdom that led to my success' (ECCLESIASTES 2:9)—for I am well versed in commerce; I know what to buy and the most prudent times to sell." . . .

This arrangement works as long as we prepare a valid garment through which the divine flow of sustenance can descend into material reality. Our occupation must be proportionate, so that according to the rules of nature the sum required for our livelihood could theoretically be gained via such an occupation. If this requirement is met, our occupation serves as a perfect garment in which G-d can disguise His blessing. . . . For we could easily claim, "I acquired this wealth through my own skills"—because it is indeed considered natural for such an occupation to yield that range of profit. Since such an assertion is logically sound, our occupation is an appropriate conduit for G-d's kindness. . . .

Accordingly, while we work, we should be mindful of our belief that our earnings are G-d's blessing; they are like any other open miracle—like the miracle of the manna. Our actions merely weave a "garment" behind which G-d can disguise His blessing. . . .

One should apply the same concept to all other areas of life. . . . Pursue your needs in accordance with your understanding, with the intention of forging an appropriate "garment" through which G-d will send His blessing. G-d will then act as He sees fit, providing the truest form of good that is appropriate for you.

The *Sarajevo Haggadah* was copied and illuminated on vellum in Barcelona, in approximately 1350 CE. It opens with thirty-four pages of illustrations that depict biblical scenes, including this one, of the Israelites collecting the heavenly manna. The pages of this *Haggadah* are stained with wine, evidence that it was used at many Passover *seders*. This *Haggadah* survived many close calls with destruction, including the Spanish Expulsion, World War II, and the Bosnian War in 1992. (National Museum of Bosnia and Herzegovina, Sarajevo)

EXERCISE 1.3

Use the words "G-d" and "human action" to craft a single sentence that expresses how Text 11 might envision the divine-mortal interplay in matters like security.

Compare it to the sentence you created in the previous exercise.

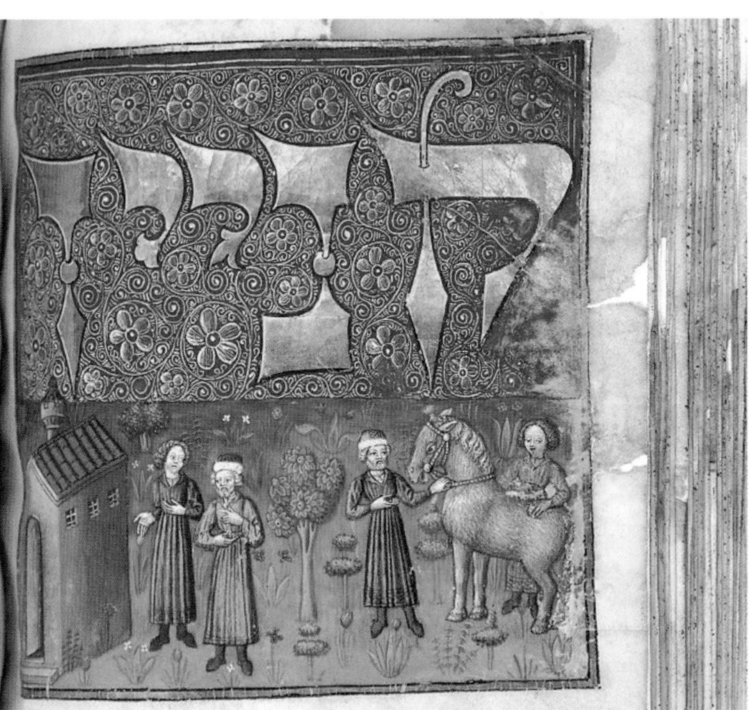

This copy of Maimonides's *Mishneh Torah* (sometimes referred to as the "Frankfort *Mishneh Torah*") was created in Northern Italy, ca. 1457. This is the first page of *Sefer Kinyan*, the twelfth volume of this legendary legal code, containing laws applicable to the economic sphere. Each book begins with a richly illuminated drawing; for *Sefer Kinyan*, the depiction is the sale of a donkey (on right) and of a home (on left). (The Israel Museum, Jerusalem; The Metropolitan Museum of Art, New York)

TEXT 12

Between “Causes” and “Garments”

The Rebbe, Rabbi Menachem Mendel Schneerson,
Likutei Sichot 31, p. 175

בְּהַנְהָגָתָהּ שֶׁל אֶסְתֵּר הֶרְאֲתָה לָהֶם בַּעֲלִיל, שֶׁהֲלִיכָתָהּ לַאֲחַשְׁוֵרוֹשׁ הִיא בְּאֹפֶן שֶׁל רַק "לְבוּשׁ" לַהַצָּלָה הַבָּאָה מִלְמַעְלָה, בְּאֹפֶן שֶׁל נֵס לְמַעְלָה מִן הַטֶּבַע. וְלָכֵן לְכֹל לְרֹאשׁ זְקוּקִים לִתְפִלָּה וְתַעֲנִית כְּדֵי לִהְיוֹת רְאוּיִים לְנֵס זֶה; אוּלָם מֵאַחַר שֶׁרָצָה הַקָּבָּ"ה שֶׁהַהַצָּלָה נִסִּית דִּלְמַעְלָה תִּהְיֶה לָהּ אֲחִיזָה בְּדַרְכֵּי הַטֶּבַע, לָכֵן צִוָּה עָלֶיהָ מָרְדְּכַי בִּדְבַר ה' לָלֶכֶת לַאֲחַשְׁוֵרוֹשׁ (וְאַף שֶׁסַּכָּנָה בַּדָּבָר).

וּבְמֵילָא מוּבָן שֶׁאֵין מָקוֹם לְהִתְחַשֵּׁב כָּל כַּךְ בְּהַ"לְבוּשׁ" (אִם אֵינוֹ בְּהֶתְאֵם לְגַמְרֵי עִם כָּל הַדָּרוּשׁ עַל פִּי דַרְכֵּי הַטֶּבַע), כִּי הָעִקָּר אֵינוֹ הַלְּבוּשׁ שֶׁבּוֹ בָּאָה הַהַצָּלָה, כִּי אִם סִבַּת הַהַצָּלָה.

Esther’s conduct demonstrated that she considered her act of approaching Ahasuerus as a mere “garment” for G-d’s salvation, knowing that it would in fact be an entirely supernatural miracle. It was therefore necessary that the Jews first pray and fast to become worthy of such a miracle. Nevertheless, because G-d desired that the supernatural salvation should appear to be within the natural order, Mordecai instructed Esther to make an appeal to Ahasuerus (despite the grave risk).

Consequently, it was not of great significance for the features of the “garment” to meet all the

RABBI MENACHEM MENDEL SCHNEERSON 1902–1994

The towering Jewish leader of the 20th century, known as “the Lubavitcher Rebbe,” or simply as “the Rebbe.” Born in southern Ukraine, the Rebbe escaped Nazi-occupied Europe, arriving in the U.S. in June 1941. The Rebbe inspired and guided the revival of traditional Judaism after the European devastation, impacting virtually every Jewish community the world over. The Rebbe often emphasized that the performance of just one additional good deed could usher in the era of Mashiach. The Rebbe’s scholarly talks and writings have been printed in more than 200 volumes.

demands of the natural order. For the primary concern was not the *medium* through which G-d's salvation would arrive, but rather, the need to ensure that the *cause* for salvation had been secured.

This drawing is from a *Megillah* written and illustrated by Moshe ben Avraham Peshkarol in Ferrara, Italy. It is one of the earliest extant *Megillot*, dating back to 1616. It features lavish marginalia depicting Esther's story as illuminated by Midrashic sources, along with faunal and floral motifs. Presented here is a depiction of Ahasuerus's first feast. From the collection of the National Library of Israel, courtesy of Center for Jewish Art at the Hebrew University of Jerusalem

TEXT 13

Thinking and Doing

The Rebbe, Rabbi Menachem Mendel Schneerson,
Sefer Hasichot 5750:2, pp. 413–415

זֶה עַתָּה (כְּשָׁעָה לְעֶרֶךְ לִפְנֵי תְּפִלַּת מִנְחָה) נִתְקַבְּלָה יְדִיעָה שֶׁאִרְגּוּן אַשַ"ף פִּירְסֵם הוֹרָאָה לְכָל הַמַּחְלָקוֹת שֶׁלּוֹ בְּרַחֲבֵי הָעוֹלָם לִפְגּוֹעַ בְּשׂוֹנְאֵי יִשְׂרָאֵל (בְּלָשׁוֹן סַגִּי נָהוֹר), הָיָה לֹא תִהְיֶה, פְּגִיעָה בְּגוּף וְכוּ' וְכוּ', אֲשֶׁר, אֵין לְהַאֲרִיךְ בָּזֶה מִשּׁוּם "אַל תִּפְתַּח פֶּה כוּ'".

וְלָכֵן, יֵשׁ צוֹרֶךְ לְהַדְגִּישׁ בִּמְיוּחָד בִּרְכוֹתָיו שֶׁל הַקָּבָּ"ה לְכָל בְּנֵי יִשְׂרָאֵל בְּכָל מָקוֹם שֶׁהֵם בְּכָל הַמִּצְטָרֵךְ לָהֶם, מִתּוֹךְ הַרְחָבָה, בְּבִטָּחוֹן אֲמִיתִּי, וּמִתּוֹךְ שִׂמְחָה וְטוּב לֵבָב, כּוֹלֵל וּבִמְיוּחָד - קִיּוּם הַהוֹרָאָה הַיְדוּעָה "טְרַאכְט גוּט וֶועט זַיין גוּט", הַיְינוּ, שֶׁהַמַּחְשָׁבָה לְטוֹבָה פּוֹעֶלֶת שֶׁיִּהְיֶה טוֹב בְּפוֹעַל מַמָּשׁ, וְעַד שֶׁהַקָּבָּ"ה **מַקְדִּים** הַטּוֹב בְּפוֹעַל מַמָּשׁ עוֹד לִפְנֵי הַמַּחְשָׁבָה לְטוֹבָה.

וּבְיַחַד עִם זֶה, יֵשׁ לְנַצֵּל יְדִיעָה הַנַּ"ל (לֹא בְּאוֹפֶן שֶׁל הַפְחָדָה, חַס וְשָׁלוֹם, אֶלָּא מִתּוֹךְ שִׂמְחָה וְטוּב לֵבָב, כָּאָמוּר, "לַחְשׁוֹב לְטוֹבָה") כְּדֵי לְהוֹסִיף עוֹד יוֹתֵר **בַּעֲבוֹדָתָם שֶׁל יִשְׂרָאֵל** בְּעִנְיְנֵי הַתּוֹרָה וּמִצְוֹת.

About an hour ago, I received word that the PLO commanded all of its international chapters to strike "Jewish enemies," and inflict bodily harm and much more—may it never come to be! We will not elaborate on such negative things.

It is therefore necessary to underscore G-d's abundant blessings to all Jews, in all places, for all that they need, with an attitude of happiness and authentic trust. Special emphasis should be placed on the well-known directive, "Think good and it will be good"—positive thoughts lead to positive outcomes. . . .

It is also appropriate to utilize this information—not to frighten, G-d forbid, but with a happy attitude, thinking positively—to add more in matters of Torah and *mitzvot*.

Illuminated page from the Rothschild Miscellany, a strikingly elegant Hebrew manuscript comprised of thirty-seven distinct texts accompanied by masterful artwork, crafted in Northern Italy between 1460–1480. The depiction here of a man placing his right hand on the *mezuzah* as he exits his home is featured alongside a halachic text that describes how this custom reminds us of G-d's protection. (Israel Museum, Jerusalem)

KEY POINTS

1. Worrying creates dejection and ineptitude. To address an issue effectively, we need to reduce the anxiety associated with it.

2. The Jewish people are an eternal people. History has shown that despite the pain and suffering that we have endured, the Jews and Judaism always survive and thrive. Recognizing this is an important step toward feeling optimistic about our people and about our future.

3. To be realistic means to not lose sight of the fact that we are living in one of the best eras for Jews, and we should be thankful for that. For the first time in millennia, the vast majority of Jews do not live under regimes that persecute Jews. And in some countries, while individual acts of antisemitism have risen, the data also show that fewer people overall harbor antisemitic sentiments than previously.

4. The ultimate Jewish answer to anxiety is *bitachon*. We are empowered to ingrain in our minds a trusting attitude, feeling that G-d is going to take care of us, and that He will be with us even when we pass through dark times. In fact, placing our trust in G-d triggers the opening of channels for additional revealed goodness.

5 The Torah teaches us that the success of any of our endeavors is G-d's providence and blessing. Nothing in our lives is a mere product of nature. G-d instructs us, however, to create a "garment" through which His blessings can operate in disguise. Hence, we must take all the "natural" steps, whether to earn a livelihood or to protect ourselves from antisemites, but the blessing is entirely G-d's doing.

6 Accordingly, our efforts to engage in the logical methods of protecting ourselves are inseparable from our efforts to secure G-d's protection. In the Purim story, Queen Esther recognized this, and she therefore prioritized being worthy of G-d's protection over being attractive to Ahasuerus.

The Miracle of Jewish Survival

A MESSAGE FROM DUST

Maimonides (1135–1204)

Epistle to Yemen

Cairo, 1173

G-d assured our father Jacob early on that although the nations would enslave his descendants, treat them cruelly, and subjugate them, his children would survive and endure, whereas those who enslaved them would eventually disappear. G-d told him (Genesis 28:14), "Your descendants will be like the dust of the earth." Although they are destined to be trampled and downtrodden as everyone tramples the dust of the earth, they will overcome and triumph in the end, just as, to continue the analogy, the dust eventually rises over those who trampled upon it [when their corpses are buried]. So Israel will remain in existence, whereas those who have trodden upon her will not. . . .

The Creator similarly assured us through His prophets that we will never be destroyed, that He will never permit our annihilation, and that we will never stray from being a nation devoted to its purpose. Just as it is impossible for G-d's own existence to be nullified, so is it impossible that we should be destroyed and eliminated from the world. So spoke Malachi (3:6): "I am G-d and I have not changed, and you, the Children of Jacob, have not been destroyed."

THE SCIATIC NERVE

Anonymous Author | *Sefer Hachinuch*, Mitzvah 3

Barcelona, ca. 1257

The commandment to refrain from eating the sciatic nerve serves as a hint to the Jewish people that although they will suffer many troubles in exile by the hand of the nations and the descendants of Esau, they should be confident that they will not perish. Their descendants and name will stand firm forever, and a redeemer will come and redeem them from their oppressor. By continually remembering this idea through observing this commandment, they will stand firm in their faith and righteousness forever.

This message of survival stems from the fact that the angel who fought with Jacob our forefather—who, according to tradition, was the guardian angel of Esau—wished to eliminate Jacob from the world . . . but could not overcome him (Genesis 32:26). But the angel did manage to anguish Jacob by injuring him in the area of the sciatic nerve.

Likewise, Esau's seed anguishes the seed of Jacob; but in the end, Israel will be saved from them.

The Torah states that the sun shone to heal Jacob and he was saved from pain (Genesis 32:32). Similarly, the sun of the Messiah will eventually shine, heal us from our pain, and redeem us speedily in our days, amen!

WHAT SHOULD HAVE HAPPENED

Rabbi Yehoshua ibn Shuib (ca. 1280–1340) | Homilies, *Parshat* Vayikra

Toledo, First half of 14th century

Even today, G-d awesomely sustains us among our enemies who hate us greatly. Indeed, a wise person once said that no hatred is as strong as the hate between nations. . . .

Our exile and persecution demonstrate the strength of Judaism and testify to the validity of our faith. Were it not for G-d's great kindness, the reality of our dispersion coupled with the nations' enmity toward us should have resulted in no remnant or memory being left of us.

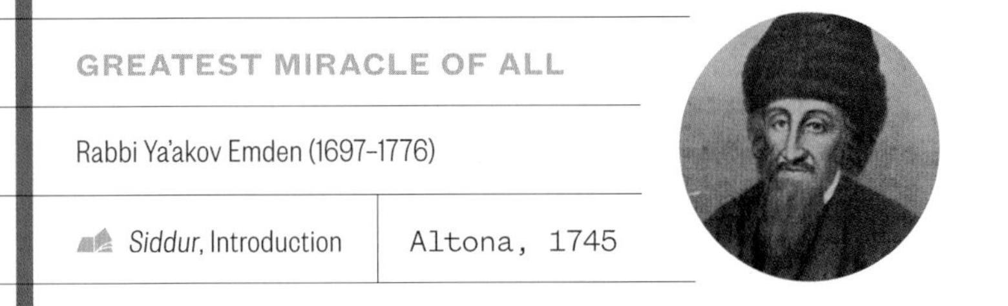

GREATEST MIRACLE OF ALL

Rabbi Ya'akov Emden (1697–1776)

Siddur, Introduction | Altona, 1745

How can those who deny providence not stand ashamed and mortified when they carefully consider the implications of our unique circumstance in the world?

We are the exiled nation, the lost sheep. Considering all the troubles that passed over us through the millennia, we must conclude that no nation in the world has been pursued as we have been. How numerous our enemies have been and how powerful those who have, from our earliest days, lifted their heads up, seeking to destroy and uproot us. Their hatred, caused by envy, has led them to trouble us greatly. But they have not succeeded in destroying us. All the mighty ancient nations—their remembrance is gone, their hope is naught, their protection has been removed. But we who cling to G-d—we are all alive today. Despite all of the force of our long exile, not one letter, not one dot has been lost from all of Scripture, and the words of the sages endure. Time has no sway over them.

How can a wise skeptic rebut this? Could it have been chance that caused all this? By my living soul! When I contemplate these wonders, they seem greater to me than all the wonders and miracles that G-d did for our ancestors in Egypt, in the wilderness, and in the Land of Israel. And the longer the exile continues, the more this miracle is verified, and the more we know its power and might!

The Miracle of Jewish Survival *continued*

FORETOLD

Blaise Pascal (1623–1662)

Thoughts, trans. W. F. Trotter (New York: P. F. Collier & Son, 1910), p. 209

In this search the Jewish people at once attracts my attention by the number of wonderful and singular facts which appear about them. . . . This people are not eminent solely by their antiquity, but are also singular by their duration, which has always continued from their origin till now. For, whereas the nations of Greece and of Italy, of Lacedaemon, of Athens and of Rome, and others who came long after, have long since perished, these ever remain, and in spite of the endeavours of many powerful kings who have a hundred times tried to destroy them, as their historians testify, and as it is easy to conjecture from the natural order of things during so long a space of years, they have nevertheless been preserved (and this preservation has been foretold).

WHAT IS THE SECRET?

Mark Twain (1835–1910)

"Concerning the Jews," *Harper's New Monthly Magazine* 99:592 (September 1899), p. 535

The Egyptian, the Babylonian, and the Persian rose, filled the planet with sound and splendor, then faded to dream-stuff and passed away; the Greek and the Roman followed, and made a vast noise, and they are gone; other peoples have sprung up and held their torch high for a time, but it burned out, and they sit in twilight now, or have vanished. The Jew saw them all, and is now what he always was, exhibiting no decadence, no infirmities of age, no weakening of his parts, no slowing of his energies, no dulling of his alert and aggressive mind. All things are mortal but the Jew; all other forces pass, but he remains. What is the secret of his immortality?

IMPERVIOUS TO THIS ALCHEMY

Arnold Toynbee (1889–1975)

A Study of History, Abridgement of Volumes I–VI (New York: Oxford University Press, 1947), p. 94

The Jews live on—the same peculiar people—today, long after the Phoenicians and the Philistines have lost their identity like all the nations. The ancient Syriac neighbours of Israel have fallen into the melting-pot and have been re-minted, in the fullness of time, with new images and superscriptions, while Israel has proved impervious to this alchemy—performed by History in the crucibles of universal states and universal churches and wanderings of the nations—to which we Gentiles all in turn succumb.

INEFFABLE WORD

Maurice Samuel (1895–1972)

The Professor and the Fossil (New York: Knopf, 1956), p. 163

As the Modern world opens, Jewry and Judaism are still very much on the scene. A fascinating historical drama is revealed. The auctioneer is Time, the buyer Oblivion. The peoples come up on the block, one after another, the hammer is lifted, the established formula is intoned: "Going! Going! Gone!" But there is one people that appears on the block regularly, and over it the words "Going! Going!" have been repeated again and again; again and again it has looked like a sale: but the third word has never been pronounced over it.

Examples of Antisemitic Tropes and Memes

BESTIALIZATION

Since ancient times, Jews have been compared in derogatory terms to barnyard and wild animals. In some influential ancient texts, for example, Jews are compared to pigs, goats, cows, and apes. In medieval Europe, Jews were often compared to pigs or depicted as having intimate relations with pigs. The term *Judensau*, which refers to obscene contact between Jews and female pigs, appeared in thirteenth-century Germany and remained popular throughout Europe for several hundred years. Snakes, rats, and octopuses are variations on this theme that remain popular today.

BLOOD LIBEL

Since ancient times, Jews have been falsely accused of killing non-Jews for ritual purposes. In medieval Europe, beginning in the twelfth century, this was often accompanied by accusations that Jews used their victims' blood to bake matzah for the Jewish holiday of Passover. Historically, these false allegations have frequently been followed by antisemitic riots and mass murders. Echoes of this blood libel can still be heard in discourse today.

COMMUNISTS

The involvement of some Jews in communist and social democratic movements in Europe has often become the basis for claims of Judeo-Bolshevism or Judeo-Communism. This myth was widespread across Europe in the first half of the twentieth century, and Nazi propaganda actively promoted it within both Germany and the territories it occupied during World War II. The internationalism of early Communism, combined with the fact that some Jewish resistance fighters joined Soviet partisan units or national Communist parties, often supplemented claims that Jews collectively or as individuals lacked loyalty to their homelands. In modern times, the trope of the communist Jew resurfaces in discussions about national identity and as claims that local crimes against Jews before, during, and after the Holocaust were the result of anti-Communist fervor.

DEMONIZATION

Beginning primarily in the fourth century, some influential figures in Christian theology have associated Jews with the devil or with demonic elements. During some periods of the Middle Ages, Jews were seen as children of the devil, portrayed with horns and bulging eyes, and associated with satanic attributes such as immense power and devious logic. In the contemporary world, these images are being resurrected in depictions of Jews, individually or collectively, bearing cosmically malevolent characteristics. This can be seen, for example, in caricatures of Jewish public figures depicted as devils or demons.

DIRT AND DISEASE

Jews have long been described by antisemites as carriers of a physical defect or disease. In some cases, these defects have been associated with Jewish masculinity or femininity—for example, in the myth of Jewish male menstruation. Similarly, the phrase "dirty Jew" and stereotypes of "Jewish odor" were once commonplace. For example, Jews were blamed for spreading the Black Death in the fourteenth century, while during the nineteenth and early twentieth centuries, racialists often perceived Jews as possessing inferior, nonwhite racial characteristics. Nazi claims that Jews spread disease also correlate with this trope. Since the mid-twentieth century, conversely, Jewishness has often been associated with a false sense of white racial superiority, sometimes associated with racism and colonialism.

DUAL OR LACK OF NATIONAL LOYALTY

Jews are often subject to claims that they conspire to shape public policy for Jewish interests, or that their patriotism is less than that of other citizens. This occasionally manifests as claims that Jews, collectively or as individuals, are not loyal to their home countries. To be accepted as national compatriots, Jews are sometimes asked to disavow their connection with Israel, despite the fact that Israel often forms a central part of Jewish identity. This myth can also appear in claims that Jews do not participate proportionally in military service or other public spheres of life in democratic states.

Examples of Antisemitic Tropes and Memes *continued*

DEICIDE MYTH

Since the early years of the Christian church, some Christians have condemned Jews for the death of Jesus and have held Jews collectively responsible for this action. The deicidal myth has reinforced the association of all Jews with traits that are imagined to accompany the killing of a messiah, e.g., supernatural powers, intransigence, and conspiratorial treachery.

MEDIA

Allegations of Jewish control over the media have been present since at least the early nineteenth century and were repeated in *The Protocols of the Elders of Zion*. In the twentieth and twenty-first centuries, individuals of presumed or actual Jewish ancestry, who may have personal influence as a result of the position they hold within a particular media outlet, have been conflated with claims of general "Jewish control" over the entire media industry. Some groups refer instead to "Zionist control" of the media. The idea asserts that these individuals act together over time in a conspiratorial manner to make decisions, but ignores the fact that many other individuals who may be similar in some way are also employed in the media industry, and that its variety, vastness, and constant development make it impossible for it to be controlled in such a way.

MONEY AND CRIMINALITY

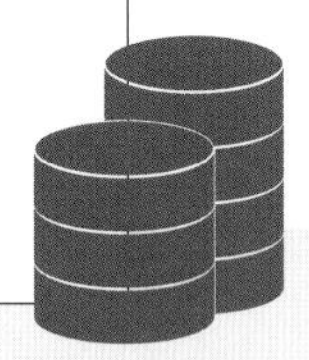

Claims of Jewish control of and fascination with finances are as old as the Christian Bible, in which Jews are occasionally portrayed as money changers engaged in unholy practice at the Temple in Jerusalem. This continued into the medieval period, when Christians were forbidden from lending money at interest, leaving the field open to others. Since Jews were severely restricted from entering most trades and from owning agricultural land, some began to lend money. Since then, Jews have been depicted as wealthy, powerful, and menacing. In some countries, Jewish women have been stereotyped as dressing ostentatiously to demonstrate wealth. Today, this trope is found in references to "Rothschild money," or the identification of a Jewish conspiracy with international banking and criminality.

RITUAL SLAUGHTER

Kosher ritual slaughter of animals for food has been depicted as a cruel, alien, and bloodthirsty practice that is linked with the underpinning belief that the Jews are in the devil's service, or with blood libel. This depiction carries over to the practice of male circumcision.

THE WANDERING JEW

Some Christian theologians have viewed Jews as a cursed people doomed to wander in misery until the end of days as testament to their depraved state. Today, there are echoes of this myth in efforts to reinforce the supposedly lowly status of diasporic Jews. This also contributes to the idea that Jews are traitorous, with no or conflicted loyalty to their homelands. This idea can also be seen in the notion that the Jews have no right to national self-determination.

WORLD DOMINATION

A pinnacle to the myth of Jews as conspirers is the idea that Jews are plotting to take over the world for their own gain. *The Protocols of the Elders of Zion*, which remains popular in reemerging editions in dozens of languages the world over to this day, is perhaps the clearest and best-known example of this theory. Today, the "The *Goyim* Know" meme is used in social media to perpetuate this theory, as are memes and articles about lizard people, the Illuminati, and the New World Order.

WELL POISONING AND DESECRATION OF THE HOST

Since the Middle Ages, Jews have been accused of tainting sacred objects or communal property. Beginning in the thirteenth century, Jews were falsely charged with reenacting the killing of Jesus by desecrating the host wafer, which was understood to represent the body of Jesus. Since that time, Jews have been repeatedly charged with conspiring to desecrate holy sites or objects. Similarly, Jews were repeatedly accused of poisoning communal wells during the medieval and early modern periods in Europe.

Source
Addressing Anti-Semitism through Education: Guidelines for Policymakers (United Nations Educational, Scientific, and Cultural Organization, 2018), pp. 80–83. Minor stylistic changes have been implemented.

LESSON 2

NO APOLOGIES

We look at some of the explanations for antisemitism that have been offered throughout the ages, to emerge with an important principle: the problem with hating Jews lies not with the Jews but with the haters. Internalizing this hate is not a healthy response.

BIRD IN A CAGE
6th-century mosaic floor.
(Ma'on Synagogue, Negev Desert, Israel)

I. ANCIENT, ABSURD, CONTRADICTORY

Antisemitism has been called the oldest hate, stretching back thousands of years. However, as the following texts demonstrate, the claims leveled against Jews were always absurd and often contradictory. This has remained true to this day.

EXERCISE 2.1

Read Texts 1 and 2. As you read, underline the phrases that feed into well-known antisemitic stereotypes and prejudices. Summarize your findings in the box that follows the texts.

TEXT 1

Tacitus Slanders Jews

Cornelius Tacitus, *The Histories*, Book V, 3–5, Loeb Classical Library Edition (Cambridge Mass.: Harvard University Press, 1931), pp. 179–183

Once during a plague in Egypt which caused bodily disfigurement, King Bocchoris approached the oracle of Ammon and asked for a remedy, whereupon he was told to purge his kingdom and to transport this race into other lands, since it was hateful to the gods.

PUBLIUS CORNELIUS TACITUS
C. 56–117

Senator and historian of the Roman Empire; considered to be one of the greatest Roman chroniclers. The surviving portions of his 2 major works, *The Annals* and *The Histories*, cover an 80-year period of the Roman Empire. Among the events documented are the Jewish-Roman War and the destruction of the Second Temple in Jerusalem.

So the Hebrews were searched out and gathered together; then, being abandoned in the desert, while all others lay idle and weeping, one only of the exiles, Moses by name, warned them not to hope for help from gods or men, for they were deserted by both, but to trust to themselves. . . .

The Jews regard as profane all that we hold sacred; on the other hand, they permit all that we abhor. . . . They first chose to rest on the seventh day . . . but after a time they were led by the charms of indolence to give over the seventh year as well to inactivity. . . .

The other customs of the Jews are base and abominable, and owe their persistence to their depravity. For the worst rascals among other peoples, renouncing their ancestral religions, always kept sending tribute and contributions to Jerusalem, thereby increasing the wealth of the Jews.

Again, the Jews are extremely loyal toward one another, and always ready to show compassion, but toward every other people they feel only hate and enmity.

Professor Jonathan Sarna explores the link between antisemitism and conspiracy theories: **myjli.com/*antisemitism***

TEXT 2

Apion Slanders Jews

Josephus, *Against Apion,* Book II, 7–9, Loeb Classical Library Edition (Cambridge Mass.: Harvard University Press, 1976), pp. 325–337

They tell lies and invent absurd calumnies about our temple, without showing any consciousness of impiety. Yet to high-minded men, nothing is more disgraceful than a lie, of any description, but above all on the subject of a temple of world-wide fame and commanding sanctity.

Within this sanctuary, Apion has the effrontery to assert that the Jews kept an ass's head, worshipping that animal and deeming it worthy of the deepest reverence; the fact was disclosed, he maintains, on the occasion of the spoliation of the temple by Antiochus Epiphanes, when the head, made of gold and worth a high price, was discovered. . . .

Now, how did it escape him that the facts convict him of telling an incredible lie? . . .

He adds a second story, of Greek origin, which is a malicious slander upon us from beginning to end. . . . In their anxiety to defend Antiochus . . . they have further invented, to discredit us, the fictitious story which follows. Apion, who is there the spokesman of others, asserts that:

JOSEPHUS
C. 37–100

Jewish historian. Born Yosef ben Matityahu Hakohen, he changed his name to Titus Flavius Josephus upon becoming a Roman citizen. His two principal works, *The Jewish War* and *Antiquities of the Jews,* are considered primary sources in documenting Jewish history during the Second Temple period. Despite surrendering his garrison to the Romans during the great revolt and later accepting Roman patronage, Josephus viewed himself as a faithful Jew.

"Antiochus found in the temple a couch, on which a man was reclining. . . . The king's entry was instantly hailed by him with adoration, as about to procure him profound relief; falling at the king's knees, he stretched out his right hand and implored him to set him free. . . . He said that he was a Greek and that, while travelling about the province for his livelihood, he was suddenly kidnapped by men of a foreign race and conveyed to the temple; there he was shut up and seen by nobody, but was fattened on feasts of the most lavish description. At first these unlooked-for attentions deceived him and caused him pleasure; suspicion followed, then consternation. Finally, on consulting the attendants who waited upon him, he heard of the unutterable law of the Jews, for the sake of which he was being fed. The practice was repeated annually at a fixed season. They would kidnap a Greek foreigner, fatten him up for a year, and then lead him to a certain wood, where they slew him, sacrificed his body with their customary ritual, partook of his flesh, and, while immolating the Greek, swore an oath of enmity to the Greeks. The remains of their victim were then thrown into a pit. The man stated that he had now but a few days left to live, and implored the king, out of respect for the gods of Greece, to defeat this Jewish plot upon his life-blood and to deliver him from his miserable predicament." . . .

Fools must be refuted, not by arguments, but by facts. . . .

Here, then, we have rank impiety at its worst, and a gratuitous lie, designed to mislead persons who do not trouble to investigate the facts.

Antisemitic motifs in Texts 1 and 2:

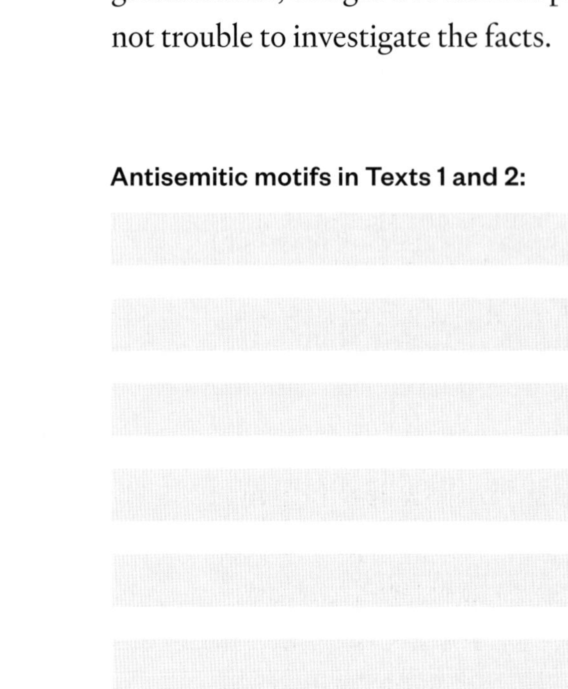

TEXT 3

Absurd in Our Day

Phyllis Goldstein, *A Convenient Hatred: The History of Antisemitism* (Brookline, Mass.: Facing History and Ourselves Foundation, 2012), pp. 343–344

Conspiracy theories are rarely logical. It is not surprising, then, that even as al-Qaeda "took credit" for the September 11 attacks, the group did nothing to stop a rumor claiming that "the Jews" were really responsible. The rumor alleged that Israel—specifically Mossad, Israel's intelligence agency—was behind the plot and had warned Jews not to go to work at the World Trade Center on the day of the attacks.

On September 18, an editor for a website known as the Information Times posted a message claiming that the "terrorist government of Israel . . . cannot be ruled out" as a suspect. The editor did not identify a motive or provide evidence in support of his allegation. In his words, he was simply raising a "reasonable question." Five days later, al-Manar, a TV station based in Lebanon, stated that Mossad had indeed warned 4,000 Jews who worked at the World Trade Center to stay home on September 11. . . . Within days, that rumor appeared in newspapers and electronic mailing lists around the world. People continued to believe the lie despite the fact that about 18 percent of the known dead were identified in obituaries as Jews.

PHYLLIS GOLDSTEIN

Educator and author. Phyllis Goldstein holds a master's degree in education from Harvard University and has worked as a teacher and author. She is the author of a number of books in the *Facing History and Ourselves* school curriculum series, including *Holocaust and Human Behavior* and *Race and Membership in American History*. Goldstein is also the author of *A Convenient Hatred: The History of Antisemitism*.

TEXT 4

Contradictory Hate

Rabbi Menachem Ziemba, *Chidushei Hagarmaz* no. 48

יֶשְׁנָם אֲנָשִׁים הַחוֹשְׁבִים וּמְנַסִים לִמְצוֹא אֶת הַנִימוּקִים וְהַסִיבּוֹת לְשִׂנְאָתָם שֶׁל הַגוֹיִים כְּלַפֵּי הַיְהוּדִים. אוּלָם הַמְצִיאוּת הוֹכִיחָה כִּי אֵין אַף סִבָּה אַחַת נְכוֹנָה, שִׂנְאָה זוֹ הִיא חַסְרַת כָּל סִיבָּה וְכָל נִימוּק אֶלָא רַק הָפַךְ לִבָּם לִשְׂנוֹא עַמוֹ.

כַּאן שׂוֹנְאִים אֶת הַיְהוּדִים עַל שׁוּם שֶׁהֵם קַפִּיטַלִיסְטִים, וְשָׁם עַל שׁוּם שֶׁהֵם סוֹצְיַאלִיסְטִים. כַּאן עַל שׁוּם שֶׁהֵם זְרִיזִים וּפִקְחִים יֶתֶר עַל הַמִידָה, וְשָׁם עַל שׁוּם שֶׁהֵם מְהַוִוים מַעֲמָסָה מִבְּלִי לְהָבִיא כָּל תּוֹעֶלֶת. כַּאן עַל שׁוּם שֶׁהֵם חֲרֵדִים וְקַנָאִים יֶתֶר עַל הַמִידָה, וְשָׁם עַל שֶׁהֵם מִתְקַדְמִים וּמְפִיצִים דֵעוֹת חִלוֹנִיוֹת.

כַּךְ תָּמִיד סוֹתְרִים הַנִימוּקִים זֶה אֶת זֶה, לְלֹא קוֹרְטוֹב שֶׁל הִגָיוֹן וְשִׁיקוּל דַעַת.

There are those who seek to identify legitimate causes for the hatred of Jews. However, reality has shown that there is no legitimate reason. Antisemitism has no justifiable cause. The haters simply choose to hate G-d's people.

This is demonstrated by the fact that Jews are hated for being capitalists—and also for being socialists. They are hated because they are overly ambitious and sharp-minded—and also because they are indolent and parasitic. They are hated because

RABBI MENACHEM ZIEMBA 1883–1943

Talmudic scholar. Rabbi Ziemba was recognized as a Talmudic prodigy from an early age. Orphaned at age nine, he was raised by his grandfather who encouraged him to become a disciple of the Gerrer Rebbe, Rabbi Aryeh Leib Alter. In 1935 he was appointed chief rabbi of Warsaw. After the German invasion, he worked to help destitute inhabitants of the Warsaw ghetto and advised on many other activities, including an underground yeshiva network. He was shot by the Nazis during the final period of the ghetto.

they are too religious and conservative—and also because they advance progressive and secular ideas.

The reasons for this hatred are consistently contradictory and have not an ounce of logic behind them.

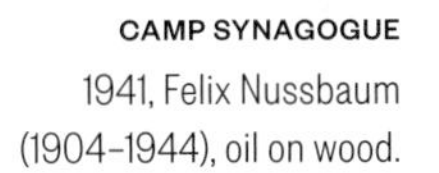

CAMP SYNAGOGUE
1941, Felix Nussbaum (1904–1944), oil on wood.

Four men wrapped in their prayer shawls stand in front of a camp barrack at the S. Cyprien concentration camp in the French Pyrenees. A single figure remains apart, perhaps alluding to his ambivalence about joining the service. Nussbaum was held as a prisoner in this concentration camp, and he executed this painting in Brussels shortly after his escape. In June 1944, Nussbaum was rearrested and was deported on the last transport from Belgium to Auschwitz-Birkenau, where he was murdered. (Yad Vashem Art Collection, Jerusalem)

II. DEALING WITH ABSURDITY

Upon reading antisemitic slanders and lies, we may be tempted to consider it sufficient to simply broadcast the correct information. While this type of effort is beneficial, it is not enough to solve the problem, because some haters simply refuse to allow themselves to be confused with facts.

A second point that is clarified by the sheer absurdity of antisemitism is that "antisemitism" is a misnomer; a more accurate term, used by Jews in prior generations, is "evil" or "wickedness."

TEXT 5

Self-Sealing Quality

Deborah Lipstadt, *Antisemitism: Here and Now* (New York: Schocken Books, 2019), pp. 7–9

It is hard, if not impossible, to explain something that is essentially irrational, delusional, and absurd. That is the nature of all conspiracy theories, of which antisemitism is just one.

Think about it. Why do some people insist that the moon landings took place on a stage set someplace in the American West? Despite the existence of reams of scientific and personal evidence to the contrary, they believe this because they subscribe to the notion that the government and other powerful entities are engaged in vast conspiracies

DEBORAH E. LIPSTADT 1947–

Historian. Lipstadt is best known as author of the books *Denying the Holocaust*, *History on Trial*, *The Eichmann Trial*, and *Antisemitism: Here and Now*. She founded the Institute for Jewish Studies at Emory University, serving as its first director from 1998–2008. Lipstadt was a historical consultant to the United States Holocaust Memorial Museum and helped design the section of the museum dedicated to the American response to the Holocaust. She is currently the Dorot Professor of Modern Jewish History and Holocaust Studies at Emory.

to fool the public. . . . If we were to provide these conspiracy theorists with evidence that proves the landing was indeed on the moon, they would a priori dismiss what we say and assume we are part of the conspiracy.

To try to defeat an irrational supposition—especially when it is firmly held by its proponents—with a rational explanation is virtually impossible. Any information that does not correspond with the conspiracy theorists' preferred social, political, or ethnic narratives is ipso facto false. Social scientists have described such theories as having a "self-sealing quality" that makes them "particularly immune to challenge."

ROBERT MICHAEL
1936–2010

Historian. Robert Michael was professor emeritus of European history at the University of Massachusetts, Dartmouth; served on the graduate faculty of Florida Gulf Coast University; and authored a dozen books on the history of antisemitism and the Holocaust.

TEXT 6

What's In a Name?

Robert Michael and Philip Rosen, *Dictionary of Antisemitism from the Earliest Times to the Present* (Lanham, Md.: Scarecrow Press, 2007), p. 292

PHILIP ROSEN
1929–2018

Historian. Philip Rosen, former educational director of the Goodwin Holocaust Museum in Cherry Hill, New Jersey, authored several books and chapters in books on the Holocaust. He served on the editorial committee of the New Jersey Curriculum Committee on the Holocaust and Genocide and taught at Temple and Arcadia Universities.

Marr, Wilhelm (1818–1904). German writer, political theorist, and agitator. In 1879, Marr founded the Antisemites' League, the first organization devoted exclusively to promoting political antisemitism. Marr's organization reflected his secular racism, which existed inconsistently alongside his religious antisemitism. His self-proclaimed goal was "to free Christianity from the yoke of Judaism." Marr coined the term *Antisemitismus*, "antisemitism," which for him denoted a secular-racial hatred of Jews. He used the word *antisemitism* to make Jew-hatred seem rational, sanctioned by science—polite.

TEXT 7

Call It What It Is

Glückel of Hameln, *Zichronot 1691–1719* (Jerusalem: Merkaz Shazar, 2006), p. 444

On the day the murderer was sentenced to death, there was a commotion in Hamburg that had not been seen there for a hundred years over any man sentenced to death; the lives of all Jews were in danger due to the extreme *rishus* [evil, wickedness] that has been roused.

GLÜCKEL OF HAMELN 1646–1724

Jewish businesswoman and diarist. Glückel was born in Hamburg to an affluent family of merchants. She was an active partner in her husband's jewelry and money-lending business, and, following his death in 1689, she continued to manage these affairs. Glückel began writing her memoirs in 1691 in order to "stifle and banish her melancholic thoughts," and to convey to her descendants their family history. These memoirs provide a rare and intimate picture of German Jewish life in the late 17th and early 18th centuries.

III. WHY?

The absurdity of antisemitism brings us to the million-dollar question: Why? Why the Jews? What can explain the existence of this ancient and absurd virus that refuses to go away?

Multiple theories abound, many of which are worthy of discussion. The following analysis of a Talmudic passage and a verse from the Book of Esther points to antisemitism as developing from a void of sorts within antisemites that makes their lives feel meaningless.

Perhaps more important than this explanation itself, or any other explanation, is the psychological canvas on which the explanation is painted. If the explanation gazes inward, blaming Jews or Judaism for the prejudices of others, the rationale is no more than an unfortunate internalization of antisemitism.

QUESTION

What might explain the persistence of antisemitism?

"The Soviet Doctor Plot"—hear from a grandchild of one of the victims: **myjli.com/*antisemitism***

TEXT 8

Multiple Explanations

Rabbi Lord Jonathan Sacks, *Future Tense: Jews, Judaism, and Israel in the Twenty-First Century* (New York: Schocken Books, 2010), p. 107

There has been an almost endless set of speculations about what the cause of antisemitism actually is.

Some have seen it in psychological terms: displaced fear, externalization of inner conflict, projected guilt, the creation of a scapegoat.

Others have given it a sociopolitical explanation: Jews were a group who could conveniently be blamed for economic resentments, social unrest, class conflict, or destabilizing change.

Yet others view it through the prism of culture and identity: Jews were the stereotyped outsiders against whom a group could define itself.

Yet others, noting the concentration of antisemitism among the very faiths—Christianity and Islam—that trace their descent to Abraham and Judaism, favour a Freudian explanation in terms of the myth of Oedipus: we seek to kill those who gave us birth.

It would be strange indeed if so complex a phenomenon did not give rise to multiple explanations.

RABBI LORD JONATHAN SACKS, PHD, 1948-2020

Former chief rabbi of the United Kingdom. Rabbi Sacks attended Cambridge University and received his doctorate from King's College, London. A prolific and influential author, his books include *Will We Have Jewish Grandchildren?* and *The Dignity of Difference*. He received the Jerusalem Prize in 1995 for his contributions to enhancing Jewish life in the Diaspora, was knighted and made a life peer in 2005, and became Baron Sacks of Aldridge in 2009.

QUESTION

Do any of these explanations resonate with you?

- Yes
- No

TEXT 9

Antisemites in Parable

Talmud, Megilah 14a

מָשָׁל דַאֲחַשְׁוֵרוֹשׁ וְהָמָן לְמָה הַדָּבָר דוֹמֶה? לִשְׁנֵי בְּנֵי אָדָם, לְאֶחָד הָיָה לוֹ תֵּל בְּתוֹךְ שָׂדֵהוּ, וְלָאֶחָד הָיָה לוֹ חָרִיץ בְּתוֹךְ שָׂדֵהוּ. בַּעַל חָרִיץ אָמַר: מִי יִתֵּן לִי תֵּל זֶה בְּדָמִים. בַּעַל הַתֵּל אָמַר: מִי יִתֵּן לִי חָרִיץ זֶה בְּדָמִים.

לְיָמִים נִזְדַּוְּוגוּ זֶה אֵצֶל זֶה. אָמַר לוֹ בַּעַל חָרִיץ לְבַעַל הַתֵּל: מְכוֹר לִי תִּילָךְ. אָמַר לוֹ: טוֹל אוֹתָהּ בְּחִנָּם. וְהַלְוַאי.

We can use a parable to gain insight into the respective positions of Ahasuerus and Haman. They are similar to two individuals, one of whom has a tall mound in his field, whereas the other has a ditch in his field. The owner of the ditch mused to himself, "I wish I could buy the tall mound to fill up my ditch." The owner of the mound said to himself, "I wish I could purchase the right to dump my mound into his empty ditch."

BABYLONIAN TALMUD

A literary work of monumental proportions that draws upon the legal, spiritual, intellectual, ethical, and historical traditions of Judaism. The 37 tractates of the Babylonian Talmud contain the teachings of the Jewish sages from the period after the destruction of the 2nd Temple through the 5th century CE. It has served as the primary vehicle for the transmission of the Oral Law and the education of Jews over the centuries; it is the entry point for all subsequent legal, ethical, and theological Jewish scholarship.

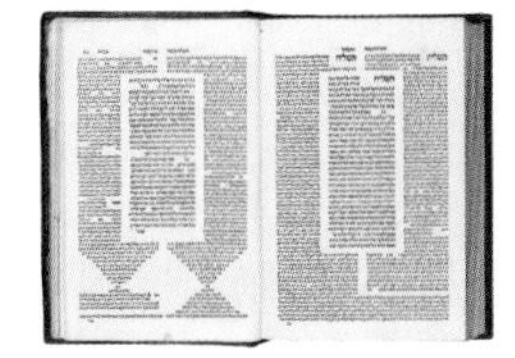

Not long afterward, the two met. The owner of the ditch said, "Sell me your mound." The owner of the mound said, "Take it for free! You'll do me a favor!"

This mid-18th-century scroll of Esther (*Megillah*) features elaborate text illustrations and ornamental motifs. The style of the painting, the various architectural and ornamental motifs, as well as details of dress and landscape, all point to a Northern Italian origin. In this drawing, Haman offers King Ahasuerus money for the destruction of the Jews. Ahasuerus raises his hand and turns his head away to refuse the money (Esther 3:9–11). (Braginsky Collection [*Megillah* 119], Zurich)

TEXT 10

When Everything Is Nothing

Esther 5:11–13

וַיְסַפֵּר לָהֶם הָמָן אֶת כְּבוֹד עָשְׁרוֹ וְרֹב בָּנָיו, וְאֵת כָּל אֲשֶׁר גִּדְּלוֹ הַמֶּלֶךְ וְאֵת אֲשֶׁר נִשְּׂאוֹ עַל הַשָּׂרִים וְעַבְדֵי הַמֶּלֶךְ. וַיֹּאמֶר הָמָן, אַף לֹא הֵבִיאָה אֶסְתֵּר הַמַּלְכָּה עִם הַמֶּלֶךְ אֶל הַמִּשְׁתֶּה אֲשֶׁר עָשָׂתָה כִּי אִם אוֹתִי, וְגַם לְמָחָר אֲנִי קָרוּא לָהּ עִם הַמֶּלֶךְ. וְכָל זֶה אֵינֶנּוּ שֹׁוֶה לִי, בְּכָל עֵת אֲשֶׁר אֲנִי רֹאֶה אֶת מָרְדֳּכַי הַיְּהוּדִי יוֹשֵׁב בְּשַׁעַר הַמֶּלֶךְ.

Haman told them about his magnificent wealth and his many sons, and how the king had promoted him and advanced him above the other officials and royal courtiers. “What is more,” said Haman, “Queen Esther personally prepared a feast, and besides the king she did not invite anyone but me. And tomorrow, too, I am invited by her—along with the king.

“But all this means nothing to me each time I see Mordecai the Jew sitting at the palace gate.”

BOOK OF ESTHER

The biblical account of the Purim story. By special request of Esther to the “Men of the Great Assembly,” this book was included in the biblical canon. The Book of Esther is read from a scroll twice on the holiday of Purim, the holiday that commemorates the Jews’ victory over their antisemitic enemies.

Mr. Robert Krakow wrote a play in which Hitler is put on trial. The witnesses called to the stand reveal the multidimensional nature of antisemitism: **myjli.com/*antisemitism***

These two drawings are presented above columns nos. 12 and 13 of a decorated *Megillah* (scroll of the Book of Esther) written and drawn circa 1610 by Moshe Pescarol in Italy. The scene in frame 12 depicts two servants bowing before Haman (Esther 3:2), who is wearing a turban and sophisticated attire. The scene in frame 13 depicts Mordecai (standing on the right, with his back turned to Haman) refusing to bow to Haman (Esther 3:2). (Gross Family Collection)

TEXT 11

Against Internalization

Rabbi Lord Jonathan Sacks, *Future Tense: Jews, Judaism, and Israel in the Twenty-First Century* (New York: Schocken Books, 2009), pp. 106–107

Jews must fight antisemitism but never internalize it. That is easier said than done. If you are hated, it is natural to believe you are hateful, that the defect lies in you. It rarely does. Hate exists in the mind of the hater, not in the person of the hated. . . . Jews have faults, and Judaism is a religion of self-criticism and repentance, but those faults have nothing to do with those of which they are accused by their enemies. Antisemitism tells us about antisemites, not Jews. . . .

One of the mistakes made by good, honorable and reflective Jews was to believe that since Jews were hated because they were different, they should try as far as possible *not* to be different.

So, some converted. Others assimilated. Yet others reformulated Judaism to eliminate as far as possible all that made Jews and Judaism distinctive. When these things failed—as they did, not only in nineteenth-century Germany and Austria but also in fifteenth-century Spain—some internalized this failure. Thus was born the tortured psychology known as Jewish self-hatred.

IV. AN OPEN IDENTITY

Jews have long struggled with the question about how open they ought to be about their Jewishness. Some Jews have felt that it is best if Judaism remains a private affair, with little to no public expression. Some have been prompted to agree to this approach out of a desire to reduce antisemitism, assuming that the public expression of Jews and Judaism triggers antisemitic sentiments.

The following texts make a case to the contrary: being open about Judaism is better for Jews and for all minorities. The story of Esther dramatically suggests that it can actually reduce the spread of antisemitism.

TASHLICH
Zalman Kleinman (1933–1995).
Tashlich, or "casting," is the Rosh Hashanah custom to recite Micah 7:18–19, which describes G-d as casting our iniquities into the depths of the sea. It is performed near a body of water, to invoke the imagery of the verse.

TEXT 12

Ethnic Conspicuousness

Rabbi Dr. Abraham J. Twerski, *Generation to Generation* (Brooklyn, NY: Traditional Press, 1986), p. 92

I was once traveling on a bus, dressed in my customary garb, wearing a broad black hat and a black frock coat. A man approached me and said, "I think it's shameful that your appearance is so different. There is no need for Jews in America to be so conspicuous, with long beards and black hats."

"I'm sorry, mister," I said to the man. "I'm not Jewish. I'm Amish, and this is how we dress."

The man became apologetic. "Oh, I'm terribly sorry, sir," he said. "I did not mean to offend you. I think you should be proud of preserving your traditions."

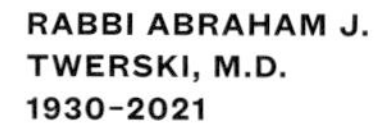

RABBI ABRAHAM J. TWERSKI, M.D. 1930–2021

Psychiatrist and noted author. A scion of the Chernobyl Chasidic dynasty, Rabbi Twerski was a well-known expert in the field of substance abuse. He authored more than 80 books on self-help and Judaism and was a pioneer in raising awareness of the dangers of addiction, spousal abuse, and low self-esteem. He served as medical director of the Gateway Rehabilitation Center in Pittsburgh and as associate professor of psychiatry at the University of Pittsburgh School of Medicine.

A card with wishes for the new year featuring a Jewish immigrant family arriving on Ellis Island, with New York's turn-of-the-century skyline in the background. (The National Library of Israel, Ephemera Collection)

TEXT 13

When Statements Are Needed

Bari Weiss, *How to Fight Anti-Semitism*
(New York: Crown Publishing, 2019), p. 172

In the first three decades of my life, I never wore a Magen David necklace. It always seemed redundant to me. But since the Pittsburgh attack, I have worn a Jewish star pendant regularly, especially in public venues and in situations where I am conscious of being one of the only Jews in the room. The show of pride has become important to me. I want people to know that I am unafraid.

This is the example set by Mitchell Leshchiner during his middle school graduation this Spring in Vernon Hills, Illinois. Leshchiner doesn't usually wear a kippah. But the Poway shooting changed things for the fourteen-year-old. "It was important to make a statement that we're still here, and that no matter what happens, we'll still be here," he said.

BARI WEISS
1984–

Opinion writer. Weiss was an op-ed and book review editor at *The Wall Street Journal* before joining *The New York Times* in 2017 as an op-ed staff editor and writer about culture and politics until she resigned in 2020. She has also served as a senior editor at *Tablet,* an online magazine of Jewish politics and culture. In 2019 she authored her first book, *How to Fight Anti-Semitism.*

TEXT 14

A Symbol Against Uniformity

Cecil Roth, *The Jewish Contribution to Civilization*
(New York: Harper and Bros., 1940), pp. 45–46

In this fact, perhaps, lay the greatest service of the medieval Jew to mankind. It was a period when authority was triumphant in the intellectual sphere,

CECIL ROTH
1899–1970

British Jewish historian. Dr. Roth was a professor of Jewish Studies at Oxford University and later served as visiting professor at Bar-Ilan University in Israel and at the City University of New York. A prolific author, he wrote more than 600 historical works on Jewish topics, such as the Dead Sea Scrolls and Jewish art. Roth served as editor of the *Encyclopedia Judaica* from 1965 until his passing.

when thought was circumscribed even more than practice, when uniformity had established itself, not as an accident but as a principle, throughout European life. Had this state of affairs continued unchallenged, progress—scientific as well as philosophical—would have been impossible.

The mere fact that the Jew existed, and that he preserved the habit of independent thought, helped to save the world from this menace. It was impossible even for the least original mind to fail to realize that in the Jewish quarter there existed a class as intelligent at least as other men were, who yet did not believe as other men, who possessed literature and beliefs and practices which were not like those of the rest of the world, and who refused to pay even lip-service to the prevailing ideas.

This very fact saved the world from accepting uniformity finally as a natural thing. It stimulated students and thinkers to realize the existence of other spheres to conquer, over and above those which were delineated from the pulpit. And, if from time to time, Europe shook off its lethargy and began to re-examine for itself the wells of human thought, the propinquity of the Jew was in part responsible.

TEXT 15

Exposing a Faulty Conclusion

The Rebbe, Rabbi Menachem Mendel Schneerson, *Torat Menachem* 5729:2 (55), pp. 332–333

וְלָכֵן הֻצְרְכָה אֶסְתֵּר רַק לְהָבִיא רְאָיָה שֶׁהַמַּסְקָנָא שֶׁ"לַמֶּלֶךְ אֵין שֹׁוֶה לְהַנִּיחָם" אֵינָהּ אֱמֶת. כְּלוֹמַר: זֶהוּ אָמְנָם "עַם אֶחָד מְפֻזָּר וּמְפֹרָד בֵּין הָעַמִּים" וְאָכֵן "דָּתֵיהֶם שׁוֹנוֹת מִכָּל עָם" . . . אֲבָל אַף עַל פִּי כֵן אַתָּה (אֲחַשְׁוֵרוֹשׁ) בְּעַצְמְךָ רוֹאֶה שֶׁ"אֵין שֹׁוֶה לְהַנִּיחָם" אֵינוֹ אֱמֶת (וְאַדְּרַבָּה - מִזֶּה מוּכָח שֶׁהַשֹּׁנִי שֶׁל בְּנֵי יִשְׂרָאֵל הוּא עִנְיָן שֶׁל מַעְלָה).

וְתֵרוּץ זֶה נִכְלַל בְּתֹכֶן דִּבְרֵי אֶסְתֵּר לַאֲחַשְׁוֵרוֹשׁ - "נַפְשִׁי בִּשְׁאֵלָתִי וְעַמִּי בְּבַקָּשָׁתִי": עַל טַעֲנַת הָמָן "לַמֶּלֶךְ אֵין שֹׁוֶה לְהַנִּיחָם" - הֵשִׁיבָה אֶסְתֵּר: דַּע לְךָ שֶׁזֶּהוּ הָ"עַם" שֶׁמִּמֶּנּוּ בָּאתִי אֲנִי (אֶסְתֵּר) . . . זֶהוּ "עַמִּי", זֶהוּ הָעָם שֶׁמִּמֶּנּוּ בָּאתִי, בּוֹ גָּדַלְתִּי וְהִתְחַנַּכְתִּי, וּמִתְנַהֶגֶת בְּאוֹרְחוֹתָיו; וַהֲרֵי אַתָּה יוֹדֵעַ שֶׁאוֹתִי בָּחַרְתָּ מִכָּל הַנָּשִׁים וְהַבְּתוּלוֹת שֶׁבְּכָל קכ"ז מְדִינוֹת מַלְכוּתֶךָ. וְאִם כֵּן יֵשׁ לְךָ הוֹכָחָה שֶׁכָּל הַטַּעֲנָה אֵין לָהּ שׁוּם יְסוֹד! . . .

אֲחַשְׁוֵרוֹשׁ יָדַע אֶת מַעֲלוֹתֶיהָ שֶׁל אֶסְתֵּר, וְיָדַע שֶׁהִיא מִתְנַהֶגֶת בְּאֹפֶן מְיֻחָד . . . וְכַאֲשֶׁר שָׁמַע מִמֶּנָּה שֶׁהַהַנְהָגָה שֶׁלָּהּ הִיא הַהַנְהָגָה שֶׁל עַם יִשְׂרָאֵל, "עַמִּי בְּבַקָּשָׁתִי" - שָׁאַל רַק דָּבָר אֶחָד: "מִי הוּא זֶה וְגוֹ'" שֶׁיָּכוֹל לְהַעֲלוֹת עַל דַּעְתּוֹ לִגְזֹר גְּזֵרָה עַל עַם כָּזֶה שֶׁמַּעֲמִיד מִתּוֹכוֹ אַחַת כְּמוֹ אֶסְתֵּר הַמַּלְכָּה?! אֵין זֶה אֶלָּא "אִישׁ צַר וְאוֹיֵב".

RABBI MENACHEM MENDEL SCHNEERSON 1902–1994

The towering Jewish leader of the 20th century, known as "the Lubavitcher Rebbe," or simply as "the Rebbe." Born in southern Ukraine, the Rebbe escaped Nazi-occupied Europe, arriving in the U.S. in June 1941. The Rebbe inspired and guided the revival of traditional Judaism after the European devastation, impacting virtually every Jewish community the world over. The Rebbe often emphasized that the performance of just one additional good deed could usher in the era of Mashiach. The Rebbe's scholarly talks and writings have been printed in more than 200 volumes.

All that Esther had to do was to prove that the *conclusion* [presented by Haman following his arguments against the Jews, namely,] that "it is not in the king's interest to let them remain," was false. She told the king: "It is true that this nation is [as Haman stated,] 'a people scattered and separated among the nations' (ESTHER 3:8). It is also true that 'their laws differ from all peoples'" [ibid.] . . . "Nevertheless, despite this," she told King Ahasuerus, "you can see for yourself that Haman's conclusion that 'it is not in the king's interest to let them remain' is not true! To the contrary, you can see that the uniqueness of the Jewish people is actually a positive quality."

This response is succinctly captured in the words Esther spoke to Ahasuerus: "May my life be given me in my petition and my people in my request" (7:3). To Haman's claim that letting the Jews live was against the king's interest, Esther responded, "You should realize that this is the nation from which I, Esther, emerged. . . . It is *my* nation, the people that produced *me*, that raised and educated *me*, and I conduct *myself* in its ways. You know well that you selected *me* from all the finest ladies, who were themselves selected from the 127 countries of your empire. If so, you have in front of you evidence that the entire complaint is without basis!" . . .

Ahasuerus agreed. He was familiar with Esther's superior qualities and exemplary behavior. . . . When he learned from her that her conduct was reflective of the conduct of the Jewish people—"*my* people"—he was left with one question: "Who in their right mind would seek to destroy a people that produces individuals as good as Esther? It could only be an evil and dangerous person!"

This drawing is from a *Megillah* (scroll of Esther) written and drawn in Italy circa 1675. At the table is King Ahasuerus along with Haman and Esther. When Esther points out that Haman wishes to destroy her people, the king is angered and leaves the room. He returns to find Haman prostrated on the ground, begging Esther to spare him. (Braginsky Collection [*Megillah* 60], Zurich)

TEXT 16

What Makes a Difference

David Horowitz, "When an Ex-Fatah Palestinian 'Neighbor' Took Up a Zionist Author's Challenge," *Times of Israel,* June 12, 2009

I started going with [my father] to [Hadassah] Ein Kerem hospital for his chemotherapy. And to my shock, I started to observe that the doctors and the nurses treated him as a patient. The doctors were very friendly and the nurses were also. He would bring them fruit, flowers and chocolate. And I noticed in the hospital that Palestinians are also receiving treatment. That actually awakened me to a great extent to the humanity in the other, and it also awakened my humanity. This was the starting point.

Illustrated compendium containing Grace after Meals and other blessings, written and illustrated by Aaron Herlingen of Geitsch, 1724. This scene depicts the medical procedure of bloodletting, along with a blessing that would be recited on such occasions. (The Library of the Jewish Theological Seminary, New York)

V. REDEEMABLE

When exploring the rationale or motivation for Jew-hatred, it is important for the explanation to include the possibility of change. For the Jewish prophets and ancient scholars insisted that antisemitism will eventually cease altogether.

TEXT 17

A Redemptive Future

Maimonides, *Mishneh Torah,* Laws of Kings 12:1

וְזֶה שֶׁנֶּאֱמַר בִּישַׁעְיָה (ישעיה יא, ו) "וְגָר זְאֵב עִם כֶּבֶשׂ וְנָמֵר עִם גְּדִי יִרְבָּץ" - מָשָׁל וְחִידָה. עִנְיַן הַדָּבָר שֶׁיִּהְיוּ יִשְׂרָאֵל יוֹשְׁבִין לָבֶטַח עִם רִשְׁעֵי עַכּוּ"ם הַמְשׁוּלִים כִּזְאֵב וְנָמֵר.

"The wolf will dwell with the lamb, the leopard will lie down with the young goat" (ISAIAH 11:6). These words are a metaphor and a parable. The interpretation of the prophecy is that the Jews will dwell at peace together with the wicked Gentiles who, like a wolf and leopard, had sought to devour them.

RABBI MOSHE BEN MAIMON (MAIMONIDES, RAMBAM) 1135–1204

Halachist, philosopher, author, and physician. Maimonides was born in Córdoba, Spain. After the conquest of Córdoba by the Almohads, he fled Spain and eventually settled in Cairo, Egypt. There, he became the leader of the Jewish community and served as court physician to the vizier of Egypt. He is most noted for authoring the *Mishneh Torah*, an encyclopedic arrangement of Jewish law; and for his philosophical work, *Guide for the Perplexed*. His rulings on Jewish law are integral to the formation of halachic consensus.

Rabbi Yosef Y. Jacobson discusses a Jewish response to antisemitism: **myjli.com/*antisemitism***

KEY POINTS

1. The absurd and contradictory claims of antisemites have persisted for millennia. Attempting to refute these conspiracy theories may keep some people away from antisemitism, but it has proven to be a futile endeavor against hard-core haters.

2. The term "antisemitism" sounds more like a theory and fails to convey that this phenomenon is actually evil wickedness.

3. Much has been said about the root cause for antisemitism. One approach sees it resulting from an inner void due to the lack of a true sense of purpose in life. The Jew represents a commitment to living for a higher purpose and dedication to the mission given to humanity by the world's Creator. Antisemites wish to obliterate their inner emptiness that they are reminded of when encountering the Jew.

4. Hatred exists in the mind of the hater, not the hated. We must avoid internalizing antisemitism and imagining that changing elements of our Jewish heritage will solve antisemitism.

5 Jews and other minorities cannot be expected to be bifurcated people, severing themselves from their identities in the public sphere. For a minority to have rights in a given place means that it can have a *public* presence. Being open about our Jewish identity benefits Jews and other minorities.

6 For some potential haters, the best antidote against stumbling into antisemitic views is knowing Jews who are upright and of noble character, and noticing that this goodness is linked to their Jewish identity, upbringing, and way of life. To have this influence, we must be open about our Jewish identity.

7 A Jewish explanation for antisemitism must allow for the possibility of change, because the Jewish prophets insisted in G-d's name that antisemitism will eventually cease altogether.

8 We can reduce antisemitism by teaching the world to avoid an inner void, by embracing G-d's mission for all of humanity.

Mapping a Deadly Lie

The blood libel, the slanderous accusation that Jews ritually sacrifice Christian children to obtain blood for their matzah, first emerged in medieval Europe in the 12th century and often led to the persecution and killing of Jews. The following map indicates two of the most famous blood libels from each century.

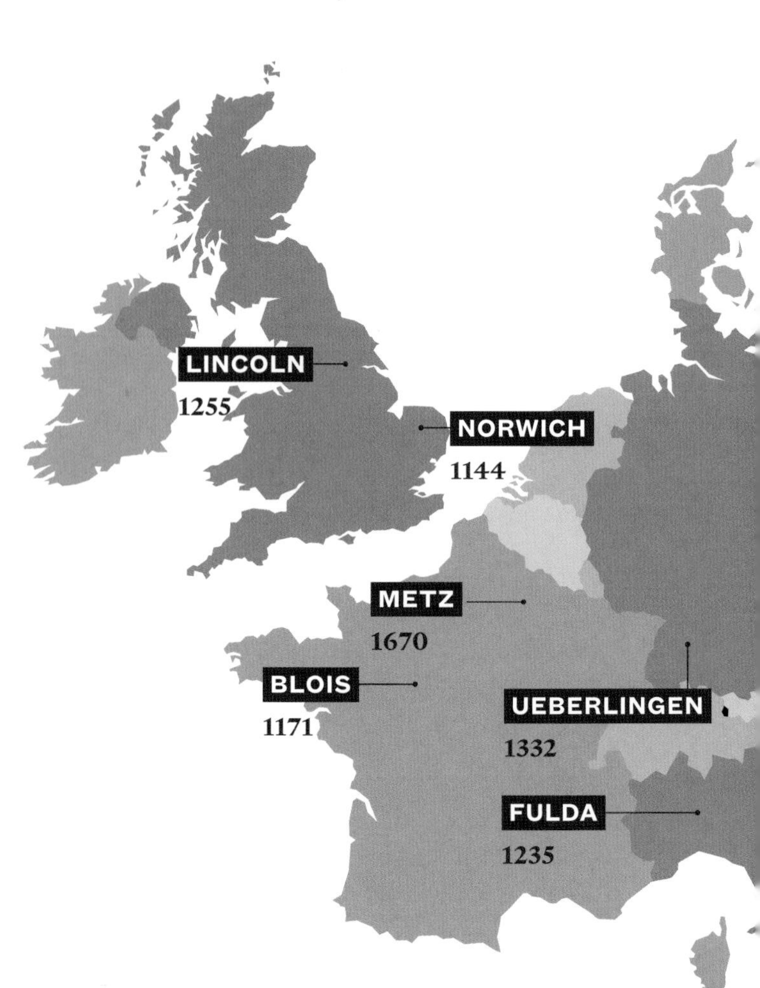

NORWICH 1144
First recorded blood libel.

BLOIS 1171
First recorded blood libel in continental Europe.

LINCOLN 1255
The first time a blood libel was endorsed by the Crown. The Jews were expelled from England 35 years later.

FULDA 1235
Jews were accused of blood cannibalism for the first time, and 34 were burned to death.

WEISSENSEE 1303
Many Jews were killed after a Christian child was found hanged.

UEBERLINGEN 1332
300 Jews were burned alive in the local synagogue.

KRAKOW 1407
The Jewish quarter was burned in riots.

TRENT 1475
The missing child Simon of Trent was beatified by the Pope, making this probably the best-known blood libel in history.

ČESKÉ BUDĚJOVICE 1505
Many Jews were killed in riots and the remainder were subsequently expelled from the city.

BAZIN 1529
30 Jews publicly burned to death, but others were spared when the missing child turned up in the meantime.

METZ 1670
Refusing to convert to Christianity under torture, the falsely accused Raphael Levy was burned at the stake, proclaiming, "I am a Jew. I wish to die a Jew."

BIALYSTOCK 1690
The alleged victim of the libel, Gabriel of Bialystock, was canonized by the Russian Orthodox Church, and his cult of veneration continues to inspire antisemitism in the area.

SANDOMIERZ 1710
A series of blood libels in the late 17th and early 18th century led to severe decrees against the local Jews.

ZHYTOMYR 1753
Jews from the area were executed and others forcibly converted to Christianity.

DAMASCUS 1840
Leaders of the Jewish community were arrested in the first blood libel in the Arab world. International pressure resulted in the acquittal of the surviving arrestees.

TISZAESLAR 1882
The eventual acquittal of the accused Jews was met by a wave of antisemtism throughout Hungary.

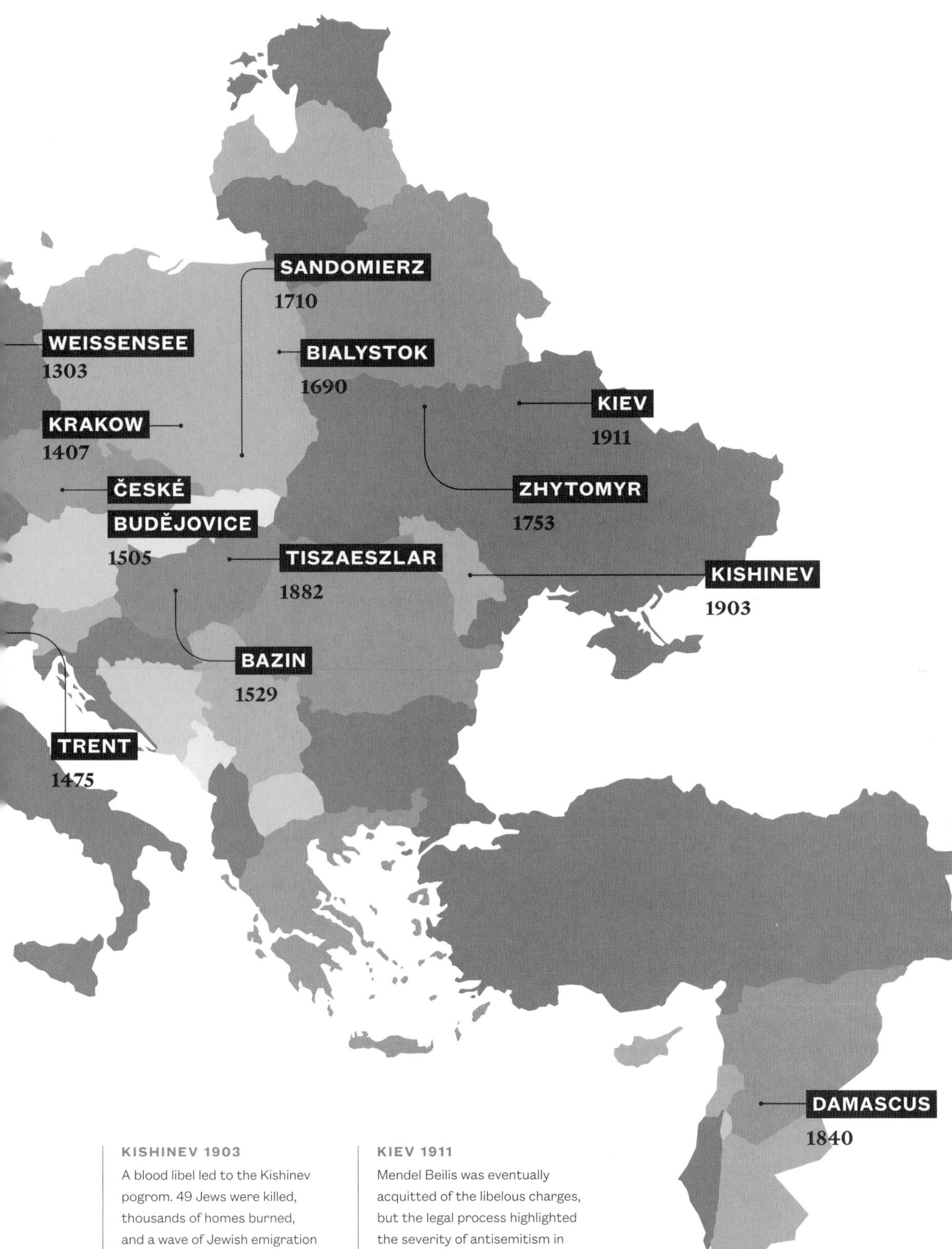

KISHINEV 1903

A blood libel led to the Kishinev pogrom. 49 Jews were killed, thousands of homes burned, and a wave of Jewish emigration from Russia began.

KIEV 1911

Mendel Beilis was eventually acquitted of the libelous charges, but the legal process highlighted the severity of antisemitism in the Russian Empire.

Chronicles of Persecution

The Jewish people have always seen great importance in remembering the persecutions they have endured. The following timeline presents a number of contemporaneous chronicles and records commemorating antisemitic persecutions and their victims.

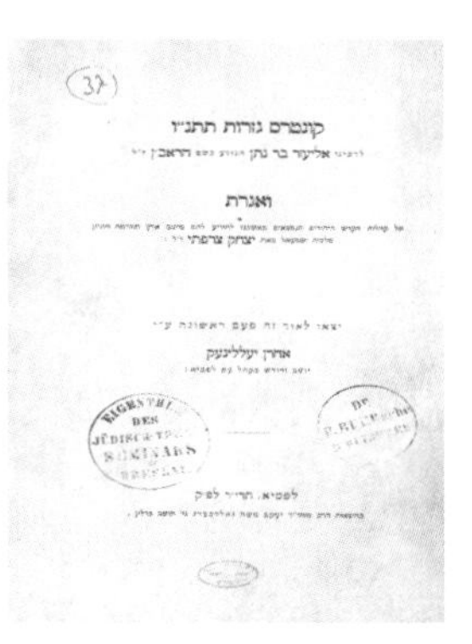

קונטרס גזרות תתנ"ו

ואגרת

יצאו לאור זה פעם ראשונה ע"י

אהרן יעללינעק

לפסיא, תרי"ד לפ"ק

1096

The Rhineland Massacres

Kuntres Gezeirot Tatn"u, Rabbi Eliezer ben Natan (Raavan)

Answering the call of Pope Urban II, in 1096 armies of knights and peasants departed on the First Crusade to conquer the Land of Israel from the hands of the Muslims. On their way to the Holy Land the Crusaders turned their attention to the "heretics" in their vicinity, massacring thousands of Jews in the German Rhineland.

Rabbi Eliezer ben Natan (c. 1090–1170) was born in Mainz, Germany and survived the massacres as a child. In *Kuntres Gezeirot Tatn"u* he recounts the story of the Rhineland Massacres based on his personal experiences and other eyewitness accounts. Rabbi Eliezer went on to serve as a leading rabbi in the Rhineland and Bohemia and authored a commentary on the siddur and a number of halachic works.

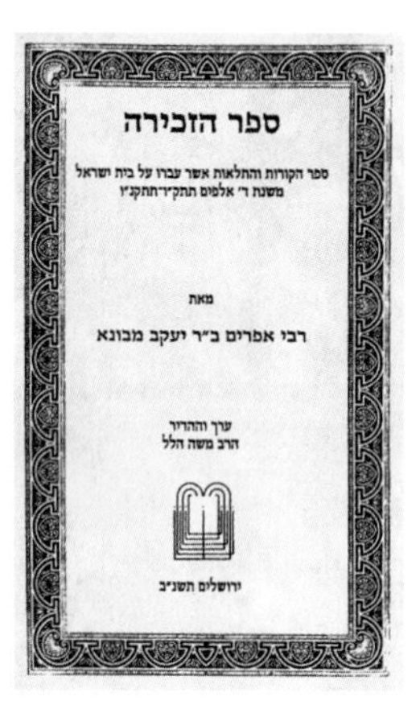

ספר הזכירה

ספר הקורות והתלאות אשר עברו על בית ישראל
משנת ד' אלפים תתק"ד-תתקנ"ו

מאת

רבי אפרים ב"ר יעקב מבונא

ערך וההדיר
הרב משה הלל

ירושלים תשנ"ב

1171

Blois Blood Libel

Sefer Hazechirah, Rabbi Efraim of Bonn

Shortly before Easter in 1171, a Christian servant in Blois, France, reported sighting a Jew throwing the body of a murdered Christian child into the Loire River. Despite no corpse being found and no child reported missing, a Christian priest pronounced the local Jews guilty and over thirty members of the community were burned alive. The blood libel of Blois was the first on the European mainland, and it was followed by many others all the way up to the twentieth century.

Rabbi Efraim of Bonn (1132–1196) was an important German Talmudist and liturgical poet. As a thirteen-year-old in 1146, he survived the pogroms against the Jews during the Second Crusade. He went on to write *Sefer Hazechirah*, a chronicle of the massacres of the Second Crusade and further persecutions and blood libels that occurred during the following three decades.

1000 1100 1200

1240

Disputation of Paris

Vikuach Rabbeinu Yechiel, Rabbi Yosef ben Natan Officiel

Fourteenth-Century Manuscript

In 1238, Nicholas Donin, a Jewish convert to Christianity, lobbied Pope Gregory IX to ban the Talmud, accusing it of being an anti-Christian work. Following the pope's call, King Louis IX ordered the Jews to publicly debate Donin about his accusations against the Talmud. Rabbi Yechiel of Paris, a leading member of the Tosafist school of Talmudic study, headed the Jewish debate team. Unsurprisingly, the Jews were declared to have lost the show trial and all known manuscripts of the Talmud were seized and burned in Paris on June 17, 1242. The Jewish record of the debate was apparently written by Yosef ben Natan Officiel, a contemporary Jewish polemicist, and published as *Vikuach Rabbeinu Yechiel.*

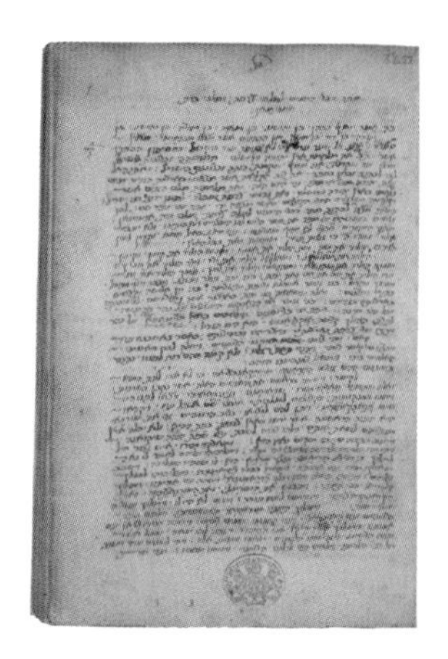

1348

Persecution of Jews during the Black Death

Emek Refaim, Rabbi Chaim Galipapa (cited in *Divrei Hayamim Lemalchei Tsarfat Ubeit Ottoman*)

In 1348 the Black Death swept through Europe killing tens of millions of people, between 30 and 60 percent of the entire population. In addition to the plague, Jewish communities were also struck by an older disease—antisemitism. Many Europeans scapegoated the Jews as the cause of divine wrath, and Jews were also accused of poisoning the wells. Together with the plague, a wave of pogroms swept Jewish communities in Spain, France, and Germany, with tens of thousands of Jews burned alive.

Rabbi Chaim Galipapa (c. 1310–c. 1380) served as a rabbi in Monzon, Spain, during the period of the Black Death, and in his book *Emek Refaim* he described in detail the pogroms that raged through city after city in the regions of Aragon, Castile, and Provence. This section of Emek Refaim is no longer extant, but key selections of it are preserved in the historical chronicle *Divrei Hayamim Lemalchei Tsarfat Ubeit Ottoman*, written by Yosef Hakohen, a sixteenth-century Jewish doctor and historian living in Italy.

1300 1400

Chronicles of Persecution *continued*

פירוש
על נביאים ראשונים
דון יצחק אברבנאל
יעקב פיראנקי
נדפס

1391
The Massacres and Forced Conversions of 1391

Letter written by Rabbi Chasdai Crescas, published in *Shevet Yehudah*

On June 4, 1391, Ferrand Martinez, a Catholic archdeacon in the province of Seville, Spain, incited a pogrom against the Jews in Seville. Over the following months a wave of antisemitic riots swept through Spain, leaving tens of thousands of Jews dead and many more forcibly baptized at the threat of death. The massacres of 1391 marked the beginning of the end for the previously successful and prosperous Spanish Jewish community, setting into motion the events that culminated in the final expulsion of the Jews in 1492.

Rabbi Chasdai Crescas (c. 1340–c. 1410) was one of the most prominent leaders of Spanish Jewry, serving as a rabbi in Barcelona and Saragossa and authoring the important philosophical work *Or Hashem*. Shortly after the massacres of 1391, Rabbi Crescas penned a heartbreaking letter to the Jews of Avignon, France, describing the massacres, in which his son was one of the many dead. Rabbi Crescas describes the feelings of the survivors: "After the dispersal of all our possessions, we have nothing left but our bodies. Throughout all this, while our hearts consider the terror, our eyes are lifted up to our Father in Heaven." This letter is published as an appendix to *Shevet Yehudah*, Shlomo ibn Verga's chronicle of the persecution against the Jews in Spain.

1492
The Expulsion from Spain

Introduction to Commentary on the Biblical Book of Kings, Rabbi Don Yitschak Abarbanel

Centuries of Jewish life in Spain came to a final end in 1492 with the expulsion of all Jews who refused to convert to Christianity. Tens of thousands left all of their possessions behind and dispersed across the Jewish world, from North Africa to the Middle East. Jews who chose to publicly accept Christianity were subject to an inquisition determined on eradicating any secret Jewish practices. Thousands of these Jewish "conversos" were burned at the stake in public autos-da-fé over the following centuries.

Rabbi Don Yitschak Abarbanel (1437–1508) was a Portuguese-born Jewish scholar who served as the financier of the court of the Catholic monarchs in the period before the Spanish Expulsion. After fleeing Spain together with his people, Abarbanel settled in Italy, where he continued his literary, business, and diplomatic activities. In the introduction to his commentary to the book of Kings, Abarbanel presents his firsthand account of the decree of expulsion, along with his failed attempts to reverse the edict.

1400 1500

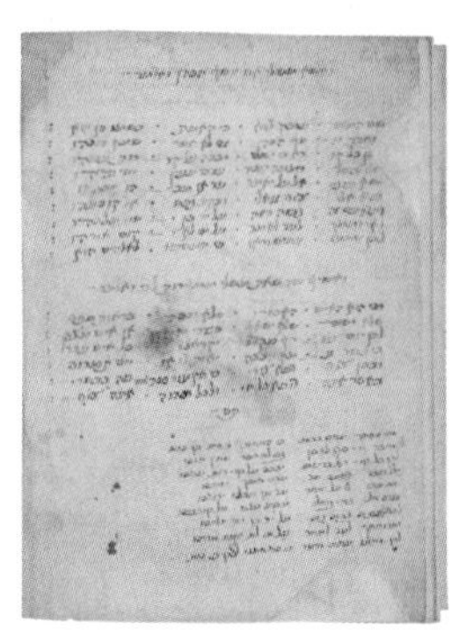

1533
The Burning of the Talmud in Italy

Emek Habacha, Yosef Hakohen
Autograph manuscript

The rapid growth of the printing business in the early sixteenth century led to intense competition among non-Jewish printers for the lucrative market of the People of the Book. Competing printers slandered each other before the Christian authorities with the charge of printing "heretical" works. After launching an investigation, Pope Julius III ordered that all copies of the Talmud be seized and burned. On Rosh Hashanah in 1533, Jewish books were burned in the center of Rome, and over the following months further public burnings were carried out across Italy. Burning the Talmud had a profound effect on Jewish scholarship, forcing Italian Jews to change their study curriculum due to the lack of available copies of the Talmud.

Yosef Hakohen (1496–1575) was born to a family of exiles from Spain and settled in Italy, where he worked as a doctor. He is best known for *Emek Habacha*, a chronicle of the history of the Jewish people and the persecutions they suffered. This work is especially valuable for the firsthand information it contains about contemporary Jewish life in Italy.

ספר יון
מצולה

1648
The Khmelnitsky Uprising

Yeven Metsulah, Rabbi Natan Nota Hanover
First Edition, Venice 1653

In 1648, Bogdan Khmelnitsky led a Cossack revolt against the Polish rule of the Ukraine. During 1648–1649, Khmelnitsky's army perpetrated horrific massacres in the local Jewish communities, killing tens of thousands and displacing many more. The trauma of these massacres, known among the Jews as *"Tach Vetat"* after the acronym of the Hebrew years in which they occurred, left a deep impression on Eastern European Jewry.

Rabbi Natan Nota Hanover (d. 1683) was living in Zaslav, Ukraine in 1648. He fled the approaching Cossack army and later settled in Italy, where he was known as a kabbalist and authored works of prayer liturgy. In 1653 he published *Yeven Metsulah*, his account of the massacres of 1648–1649 and the personal story of his escape. *Yeven Metsulah* is the primary Jewish source about these massacres.

1600 1700 1800

LESSON 3

JERUSALEM (DETAIL)
Reuven Rubin (1893–1974), oil on canvas, Jerusalem, 1925. (Beit Rubin Museum, Tel Aviv)

THE PROMISED LAND

Today, hatred of Jews commonly manifests itself as antagonism toward the Jewish State. This class distinguishes all-out antisemitism from some more nuanced substrains. It also examines the current status of Israel education and the very nature of Jewish nationhood.

I. ATTACK ON THE HOMELAND

The third segment of this course concerns antisemitism as it relates to the State of Israel. It is first necessary to clarify why so much hatred centers on Israel, and to identify methods of distinguishing between legitimate criticism of Israel and antisemitism that is camouflaged in the language of human rights. We will also explore a distinction between antisemitic movements that exclude Jews and those that invite Jews to their ranks—information that is relevant to understanding and facing opposition to Israel in the broader context of antisemitism.

TEXT 1

A Mutating Virus

Rabbi Lord Jonathan Sacks, "Future Tense—The New Antisemitism: What Is It and How Do We Deal with It?" *The Jewish Chronicle*, November 1, 2007

Antisemitism is not an ideology, a coherent set of beliefs. It is, in fact, an endless stream of contradictions. The best way of understanding it is to see it as a virus. Viruses attack the human body, but the body itself has an immensely sophisticated defense, the human immune system. How then do viruses survive and flourish? By mutating. Antisemitism mutates, and in so doing, defeats the immune systems set up by cultures to protect themselves against hatred. . . .
Most people at most times feel a residual guilt at hating the innocent. Therefore antisemitism

RABBI LORD JONATHAN SACKS, PHD
1948–2020

Former chief rabbi of the United Kingdom. Rabbi Sacks attended Cambridge University and received his doctorate from King's College, London. A prolific and influential author, his books include *Will We Have Jewish Grandchildren?* and *The Dignity of Difference.* He received the Jerusalem Prize in 1995 for his contributions to enhancing Jewish life in the Diaspora, was knighted and made a life peer in 2005, and became Baron Sacks of Aldridge in 2009.

has always had to find legitimation in the most prestigious source of authority at any given time.

In the first centuries of the Common Era, and again in the Middle Ages, this was religion. That is why Judeophobia took the form of religious doctrine. In the nineteenth century, religion had lost prestige, and the supreme authority was now science. Racial antisemitism was duly based on two pseudo-sciences: social Darwinism (the idea that in society, as in nature, the strong survive by eliminating the weak), and the so-called scientific study of race.

By the late twentieth century, science had lost its prestige, having given us the power to destroy life on earth. Today the supreme source of legitimacy is human rights. That is why Jews (or the Jewish state) are accused of the five primal sins against human rights: racism, apartheid, ethnic cleansing, attempted genocide and crimes against humanity.

FIGURE 3.1

Mutating Hate

ERA	MOST PRESTIGIOUS SOURCE OF AUTHORITY	ANTISEMITIC CLAIMS
Classical era and Middle Ages	Religion	Judaism is the enemy of the true religion.
Nineteenth Century	Science	The inferior Jewish race is infecting the superior Aryan race.
Late Twentieth Century	Human Rights	Jews violate human rights.

The *Barcelona Haggadah* was copied and illuminated on parchment in Catalonia in approximately 1340 CE. Its folios abound in illustrations depicting Passover rituals, biblical and Midrashic episodes, and symbolic foods. This page features the stirring words recited at the end of the Passover *seder*, highlighting the timeless connection between Jews and their ancestral homeland, "Next year in Jerusalem!" (British Library [MS 14761], London)

FIGURE 3.2

Pro-Israel, Yet Critical

The Mellman Group, 2018, Memo to Jewish Electorate Institute

Which of the following best describes you? Are you...

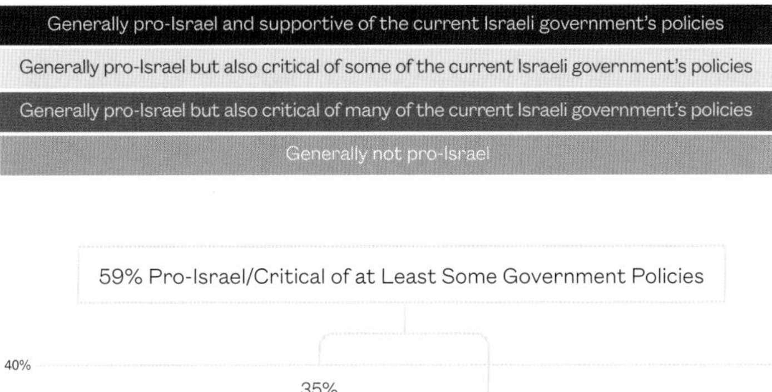

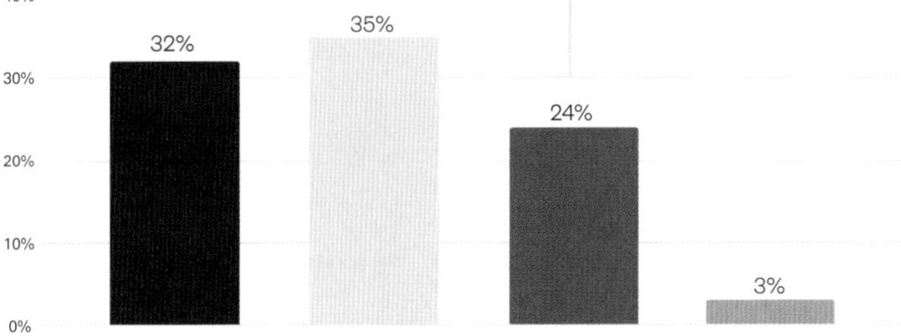

QUESTION

How might we differentiate between legitimate criticism of Israel, and criticism motivated by antisemitism?

Harvard Professor **Ruth Wisse** discusses the complexities of the Arab war against the Jews: **myjli.com/*antisemitism***

TEXT 2

Double Standard

Midrash, *Kohelet Rabah* 2:21

אִימִיקַנְטְרוֹן הָיָה כּוֹתֵב לְאַדְרִיָאנוֹס קֵיסָר: אָמַר לוֹ אִם לַמּוּלִים אַתְּ שׂוֹנֵא, אֵלּוּ הַיִּשְׁמְעֵאלִים. אִם לִמְשַׁמְּרֵי שַׁבָּת אַתְּ שׂוֹנֵא, אֵלּוּ הַכּוּתִים. הֲרֵי אֵין אַתְּ שׂוֹנֵא אֶלָּא הָאֻמָּה הַזֹּאת בִּלְבַד, אֱלֹקֶיהָ יִפָּרַע מֵאוֹתוֹ הָאִישׁ.

Imikantron wrote to Emperor Hadrian, "If it is circumcision that you hate, Arabian tribes also circumcise.

"If it is Shabbat observance that you despise, the Cutheans similarly observe Shabbat.

"Clearly, then, you simply hate the Jewish people.

"Their G-d will exact punishment from you."

KOHELET RABAH

A Midrashic text on the Book of Ecclesiastes. Midrash is the designation of a particular genre of rabbinic literature. The term "Midrash" is derived from the root *d-r-sh,* which means "to search," "to examine," and "to investigate." This particular Midrash provides textual exegeses and develops and illustrates moral principles. It was first published in Pesaro, Italy, in 1519, together with 4 other Midrashic works on the other 4 biblical *Megillot*.

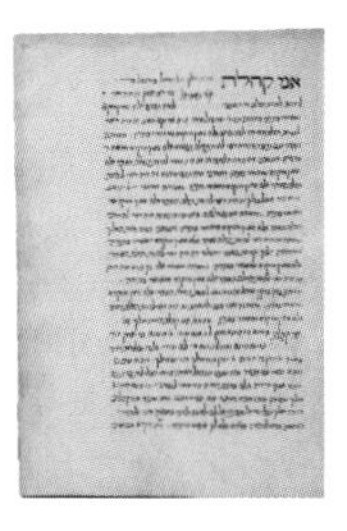

Hadrian's oppressive rule in the Holy Land triggered the Bar Kochba Revolt (ca. 132–136 CE), which Hadrian ultimately repressed with brutal force. During the revolt's initial successes, Jews minted their own coins. On one side of this silver shekel is the Jerusalem Temple facade surrounding the Ark of the Covenant; on the reverse there is a *lulav* and *etrog* with the words, "To the freedom of Jerusalem."

TEXT 3

The 3D Test

Natan Sharansky, "3D Test of Anti-Semitism: Demonization, Double Standards, Delegitimization," *Jewish Political Studies Review* 16:3-4, Fall 2004

I believe that we can apply a simple test—I call it the "3D" test—to help us distinguish legitimate criticism of Israel from anti-Semitism.

The first "D" is the test of demonization. When the Jewish state is being demonized; when Israel's actions are blown out of all sensible proportion; when comparisons are made between Israelis and Nazis and between Palestinian refugee camps and Auschwitz—this is anti-Semitism, not legitimate criticism of Israel.

The second "D" is the test of double standards. When criticism of Israel is applied selectively; when Israel is singled out by the United Nations for human rights abuses while the behavior of known and major abusers, such as China, Iran, Cuba, and Syria, is ignored; when Israel's Magen David Adom, alone among the world's ambulance services, is denied admission to the International Red Cross—this is anti-Semitism.

The third "D" is the test of delegitimization: When Israel's fundamental right to exist is denied—alone among all peoples in the world—this too is anti-Semitism.

NATAN SHARANSKY
1948–

Former Soviet dissident and Israeli politician. Sharansky is the chairman of the Jewish Agency. He spent years in Soviet prison as a political prisoner for his human rights activism. He was released after his wife led an international campaign for his freedom. He has served in various ministerial positions, and as deputy prime minister in the Israeli government.

FIGURE 3.3

The Three D Test

DDD		EXAMPLES
D	**DEMONIZATION**	Comparisons to Nazis, depicting Israel as the devil incarnate, attributing to Israel mythical powers of control over the world.
D	**DOUBLE STANDARDS**	When China, Iran, Cuba, Syria, etc., are ignored, and Israel alone is targeted as an abuser; or the fact that Article 49(6) has only been applied to Israel (see further, p. 108).
D	**DELEGITIMIZATION**	When Israel's right to exist as a Jewish state is denied.

Journalist **Yaakov Katz** explains what the media gets wrong about Israel: **myjli.com/*antisemitism***

TEXT 4

Two Forms of Antisemitism

Dara Horn, "The Cool Kids," *Tablet Magazine*, September 6, 2019

DARA HORN, PHD
1977–

Novelist and professor of literature. Dr. Horn received her degree in comparative literature from Harvard University in 2006, studying Hebrew and Yiddish. She has written multiple award-winning novels and taught courses in Jewish literature and Israeli history.

Hanukkah anti-Semitism . . . doesn't demand dead or expelled Jews, at least not at first. Instead, it demands the destruction of Jewish civilization. This process requires not dead Jews, but Jews who are willing to give up whatever specific aspect of Jewish civilization is deemed to be uncool.

Of course, Judaism has always been uncool . . . which is why cool people find it so threatening—and why Jews who are willing to become cool are absolutely necessary to Hanukkah-style anti-Semitism's success. In the days of Antiochus, this type of anti-Semitism needed those boys who voluntarily underwent painful genital surgery to prove that Jews weren't the problem—just the barbarity of Jewish law. . . .

Hanukkah-style anti-Semitism always promises Jews a kind of nobility, offering them the opportunity to cleanse themselves of whatever the people around them happen to find revolting. The Jewish traits designated as repulsive vary by country and time period, but they invariably contradict the specific values that the surrounding culture has embraced as "universal." . . .

Thanks to Judaism's inherent uncoolness, there will never be a shortage of Jews willing to comply.

II. ISRAEL EDUCATION

What is the Jewish claim to the Land of Israel? Jewish educators need to carefully consider and gain clarity on this issue, because they are positioned to greatly influence future Jewish generations' perceptions on the subject.

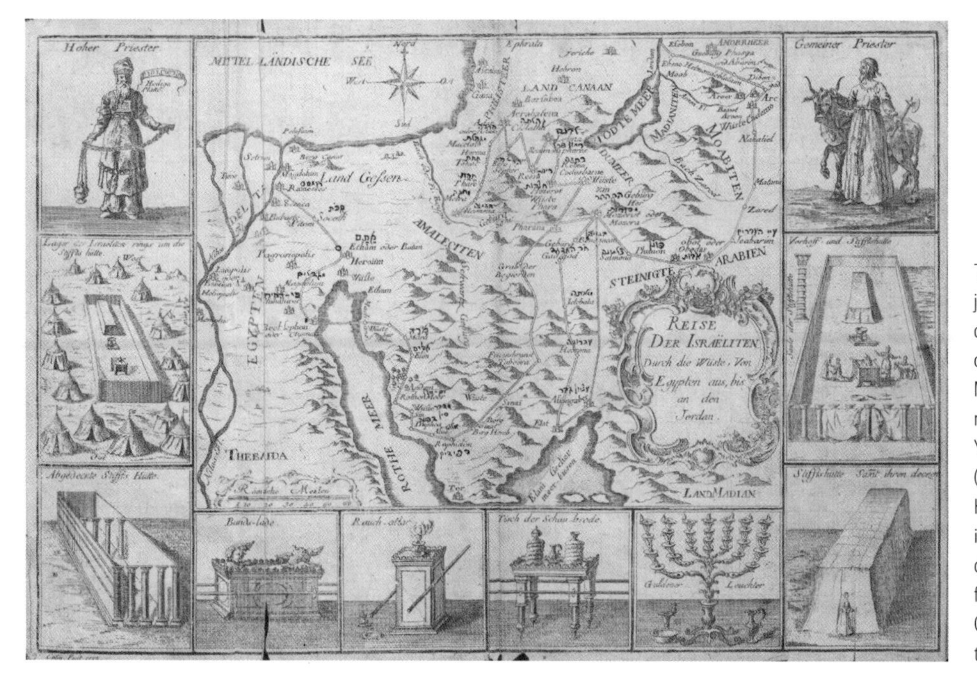

This map, depicting the Israelite journey from Egypt into the Land of Israel, was printed in the back of the 1767 *Haggadah* printed at Metz. The names of places are recorded in German, and Rabbi Yosef Yitschak Schneersohn (1880–1950) wrote by hand their Hebrew equivalents. The map is surrounded by images of the desert Tabernacle and its sacred furniture. (Property of Agudas Chasidei Chabad, currently at the Russian State Library)

EXERCISE 3.1

What is the basis of the Jewish right to Israel? List three commonly cited reasons, in the order of frequency with which they are encountered.

Epitaph of King Uzziah of Judah (who ruled in the 8th century BCE), carved into limestone presumably during the 1st century BCE. The Aramaic text reads:
לכה התית—To this place were brought
טמי עוזיה—the bones of Uzziah
מלך יהודה—king of Judah
ולאלמפתח—Do not open
(Israel Museum, Jerusalem)

TEXT 5

Turned Off by Colonialism

Phyllis Bennis, "I'm Jewish. I Fight Anti-Semitism and I Support Palestinian Rights," *Los Angeles Times*, December 2019

When I was a Jewish kid growing up in suburban Los Angeles, we thought being Jewish meant supporting Israel.

There really wasn't a choice. If you identified as Jewish, as I and most of my friends did, the religious education we got, the youth groups we joined, and the summer camps where we played were all grounded in one thing. It wasn't G-d—it was Zionism, the political project of settling Jewish people in Israel. . . .

My own break with Zionism came in my mid-20s, after reading the letters of Zionism's founder, Theodor Herzl, imploring Cecil Rhodes, the leader of British land theft in Africa, to support his work in Palestine. Their projects were both "something colonial," Herzl assured Rhodes.

PHYLLIS BENNIS
1951–

Political activist. Bennis focuses mainly on issues related to the Middle East and the United Nations, and is a prominent critic of Israel and the United States. She is involved in many organizations that seek to undermine the State of Israel.

TEXT 6

Responsive Opening

Rashi, Genesis 1:1

אָמַר רַבִּי יִצְחָק: לֹא הָיָה צָרִיךְ לְהַתְחִיל אֶת הַתּוֹרָה
אֶלָּא מֵ"הַחוֹדֶשׁ הַזֶּה לָכֶם" (שְׁמוֹת יב, ב), שֶׁהִיא מִצְוָה
רִאשׁוֹנָה שֶׁנִּצְטַוּוּ יִשְׂרָאֵל. וּמַה טַּעַם פָּתַח בִּבְרֵאשִׁית?

מִשּׁוּם "כֹּחַ מַעֲשָׂיו הִגִּיד לְעַמּוֹ, לָתֵת לָהֶם נַחֲלַת
גּוֹיִם" (תְּהִלִּים קיא, ו). שֶׁאִם יֹאמְרוּ אוּמּוֹת הָעוֹלָם
לְיִשְׂרָאֵל: "לִסְטִים אַתֶּם! שֶׁכְּבַשְׁתֶּם אַרְצוֹת שִׁבְעָה
גוֹיִם", הֵם אוֹמְרִים לָהֶם: "כָּל הָאָרֶץ שֶׁל הַקָּדוֹשׁ
בָּרוּךְ הוּא הִיא. הוּא בְּרָאָהּ וּנְתָנָהּ לַאֲשֶׁר יָשַׁר בְּעֵינָיו.
בִּרְצוֹנוֹ נְתָנָהּ לָהֶם, וּבִרְצוֹנוֹ נְטָלָהּ מֵהֶם וּנְתָנָהּ לָנוּ".

Rabbi Yitschak stated: The Torah should have begun with the first mitzvah commanded to the Jewish people, which is contained in the verse, "This month shall be to you, etc." (EXODUS 12:2). For what purpose does it start with, "In the beginning, G-d created the heavens and the earth"? . . .

The solution is found in the verse, "He recounted the strength of His works to His people, to give them the inheritance of nations" (PSALMS 111:6). In other words, if the nations of the world accuse the Jews with the claim, "You are thieves for having conquered the lands of the seven nations," the Jews should reply, "The entire world is G-d's. He created it and granted it to

RABBI SHLOMO YITSCHAKI (RASHI) 1040–1105

Most noted biblical and Talmudic commentator. Born in Troyes, France, Rashi studied in the famed *yeshivot* of Mainz and Worms. His commentaries on the Pentateuch and the Talmud, which focus on the straightforward meaning of the text, appear in virtually every edition of the Talmud and Bible.

whomever He desired. It was His will to initially give it to the seven nations, and it was His will to subsequently remove it from them and give it to us."

This page from the Pentateuch, with Rashi's commentary to the left of the biblical text, was handwritten on parchment between 1350–1399 by Mordechai Emendante. Created in Germany, it consists of 636 folios, totaling 1272 pages. It was purchased by the British Museum from N. Rabinowitz in 1883. Shown here is the first page of the Torah, with the first comment by Rashi about the link of Genesis 1:1 to the Jewish claim over the Holy Land. (British Museum [*Pentateuch, Oriental Manuscripts, Or 2696*], London)

TEXT 7

Eternal Covenant

Genesis 13:14–15

וַה' אָמַר אֶל אַבְרָם . . . שָׂא נָא עֵינֶיךָ וּרְאֵה מִן הַמָּקוֹם אֲשֶׁר אַתָּה שָׁם, צָפֹנָה וָנֶגְבָּה וָקֵדְמָה וָיָמָּה. כִּי אֶת כָּל הָאָרֶץ אֲשֶׁר אַתָּה רֹאֶה לְךָ אֶתְּנֶנָּה וּלְזַרְעֲךָ עַד עוֹלָם.

G-d told Abram . . . "Raise your eyes and look around from where you are, to the north and south, to the east and west. All the land that you see I will give to you and your offspring forever."

ABRAHAM AND THE STARS
Carol Racklin-Siegel (Oakland, Calif.: EKS Publishing, 2004), dyes on silk

TEXT 8

Winning Argument

The Rebbe, Rabbi Menachem Mendel Schneerson, *Igrot Kodesh* 26, p. 167

וָואס הָאט אִיר (הַכַּוָּנָה אֵלַי) זִיךְ צוּגֶעטְשֶׁעפְּעט צוּ אֶרֶץ יִשְׂרָאֵל אוּן צוּ אֶרֶץ הַקֹּדֶשׁ אוֹ צוּ בְּרִית בֵּין הַבְּתָרִים וְכוּ', אוּן מִישְׁט אַרַיְין דֶעם אוֹיְבֶּערְשְׁטֶען וְכוּ' וְכוּ' - הֲרֵי כָּל אֵלֶה שֶׁהִשְׁתַּדְּלוּ בָּזֶה וְכָל אֵלֶה שֶׁעָמְדוּ וְעוֹמְדִים עַתָּה בְּרֹאשָׁהּ וְכָל אֵלֶה הַמְדַבְּרִים בִּשְׁמָהּ אוֹמְרִים וּמַדְגִּישִׁים וּמַכְרִיזִים שֶׁזֶהוּ מְדִינָה שֶׁנִתְיַסְדָה בִּשְׁנַת תש"ח . . .

פָּשׁוּט שֶׁהַמַּעֲנֶה שֶׁלִּי הוּא - לֹא הָיוּ דְבָרִים מֵעוֹלָם. אֵין הַנִּזְכָּר לְעֵיל עִנְיָן חָדָשׁ וְכוּ' כִּי אִם אֲשֶׁר בִּשְׁנַת תש"ח שִׁחְרְרוּ חֵלֶק חָשׁוּב מֵאֶרֶץ יִשְׂרָאֵל . . .

דָּבָר שֶׁנִּתְיַסֵּד בְּתש"ח בְּרָצוֹן אוֹ בְּאִשּׁוּר אֻמּוֹת הָעוֹלָם - אֵין בּוֹ כָּל תֹּקֶף וְתֹכֶן לַעֲנוֹת עַל טַעֲנוֹת הָעַרְבִיִּים, הַוָּאטִיקָן, הָאֻמּוֹת הַמְאֻחָדוֹת, וְכוּ', וְהַכְּנַעֲנִיִּים (הַגְּלוּיִים וְשֶׁבַּסֵּתֶר) שֶׁמִּבְּנֵי יִשְׂרָאֵל: לִסְטִים אַתֶּם שֶׁכְּבַשְׁתֶּם אַרְצוֹת כו'.

אֵינִי מַשְׁלֶה אֶת עַצְמִי שֶׁבְּטַעֲנוֹת צֶדֶק וְיוֹשֶׁר יְנַצְּחוּ בְּאֻמּוֹת הַמְאֻחָדוֹת, בְּוַאטִיקָן וְכוּ' - אֲבָל גּוֹרֵם הָכִי חָשׁוּב הוּא בְּהַמּוֹרָל שֶׁל הַנּוֹעַר (כּוֹלֵל - דְּהַצָּבָא הֲגָנָה לְיִשְׂרָאֵל), הַסְטוּדֶנְטִים דְּאַרְצוֹת הַבְּרִית (וּבֶטַח גַּם שְׁאַר אֲרָצוֹת) וְכוּ'.

I have received complaints: Why do I invoke "the biblical Land of Israel," "the Holy Land," and the Covenant with Abraham [in connection with modern Israel]? Why do I mix G-d into the picture? After all, they say, those who fought

RABBI MENACHEM MENDEL SCHNEERSON 1902–1994

The towering Jewish leader of the 20th century, known as "the Lubavitcher Rebbe," or simply as "the Rebbe." Born in southern Ukraine, the Rebbe escaped Nazi-occupied Europe, arriving in the U.S. in June 1941. The Rebbe inspired and guided the revival of traditional Judaism after the European devastation, impacting virtually every Jewish community the world over. The Rebbe often emphasized that the performance of just one additional good deed could usher in the era of Mashiach. The Rebbe's scholarly talks and writings have been printed in more than 200 volumes.

for the creation of the state, those who led it, those who currently direct it, and its authorized representatives—they all proclaim and take pains to emphasize that Israel is a state founded in 1948. . . .

My answer, put frankly, is that their narrative is false. No new entity was created in 1948. Rather, that was the year in which a large part of the *Land of Israel* was *liberated*. . . .

An entity established in 1948 based on the agreement or authorization of the nations of the world has no strength or justification in terms of an authentic response to the claim, "You are thieves for having conquered lands belonging to others," etc., a claim raised by the Arabs, the Vatican, the United Nations, and some Jews as well. [This is why it is so crucial to underscore that it is our *G-d*-given homeland.]

Now, I do not delude myself into imagining that these just and honest arguments will prevail in the United Nations, the Vatican, etc. Nevertheless, transmitting this truth is critical for the morale of Jewish youth [living in the Holy Land], including those serving in the IDF, for Jewish American students, and for the Jewish youth of other countries as well.

Ambassador **Danny Danon** teaches the UN a history lesson on the Jewish connection to the Land of Israel: **myjli.com/*antisemitism***

III. A DEEPER CLAIM

Judaism teaches that there is a deeper spiritual reality behind every phenomenon of the natural world, including the affairs of humanity. The voices (Jewish or otherwise) that loudly question the Jewish claim to the Jewish homeland are no exception to this principle. The spiritual reality that lurks (unknowingly) behind their argument is this: If Jewish identity is rooted in the Torah's *spiritual* practices, what need is there to own a *physical* territory? This challenge is completely valid, but it invites an even more valid response.

TEXT 9

Nationhood

Rabbi Saadia Ga'on, *Emunot Vede'ot* 3:7

אוּמָּתֵינוּ בְּנֵי יִשְׂרָאֵל אֵינָהּ אוּמָּה אֶלָּא בְּתוֹרוֹתֶיהָ.

The Jewish nation is only a nation through its Torah.

RABBI SAADIA GA'ON (RASAG)
882–942 CE

Rabbinic scholar, philosopher, and exegete. Rabbi Saadia Ga'on was born in Egypt and came to the forefront of the rabbinic scene through his active opposition to Karaism, a divergent sect that denied the divinity of the Oral Law. In 928, the exilarch David ben Zakai invited him to head the illustrious yeshiva in Sura, Babylonia, thereby bestowing upon him the honorific title "Ga'on." He is renowned for his works on the Torah, Hebrew linguistics, and Jewish philosophy, and his redaction of a siddur.

TEXT 10

The Secret of Jewish Immortality

The Rebbe, Rabbi Menachem Mendel Schneerson,
Igrot Kodesh 15, pp. 446–449

סְקִירָה אוֹבְּיֶיקְטִיבִית, לְלֹא דֵעָה קְדוּמָה, לְאוֹרֶךְ הַהִיסְטוֹרְיָה שֶׁל עַם יִשְׂרָאֵל, מוּכְרַחַת לְהָבִיא לִידֵי מַסְקָנָא, שֶׁקִּיּוּמוֹ שֶׁל עַמֵּנוּ בְּוַדַּאי אֵינוֹ קָשׁוּר בְּשֶׁפַע חוּמְרִי אוֹ עוֹצְמָה פִיזִית. אֲפִילוּ בַּזְּמַנִּים הַטּוֹבִים בְּיוֹתֵר, תַּחַת הַמַּמְלָכָה הַמְאוּחֶדֶת שֶׁל שְׁלֹמֹה הַמֶּלֶךְ, הָיָה עַם יִשְׂרָאֵל וּמַלְכוּת יִשְׂרָאֵל - מִבְּחִינָה פּוֹלִיטִית וְכַלְכָּלִית - קְטַנִּים בְּהַשְׁוָואָה לְמַלְכוּיוֹת הָעוֹלָם בַּזְּמַן הַהוּא, מִצְרַיִם, אַשּׁוּר וּבָבֶל.

כְּמוֹ כֵן בָּרוּר, שֶׁלֹּא שִׁלְטוֹן הַמְלוּכָה וְלֹא הַשֶּׁטַח הַגֵּיאוֹגְרָפִי הִבְטִיחוּ אֶת קִיּוּמֵנוּ, כִּי הַהִיסְטוֹרְיָה שֶׁלָּנוּ בְּתוֹר עַם בַּעַל מְדִינָה בְּאַרְצוֹ, הִיא קְצָרָה בְּיוֹתֵר בְּהַשְׁוָואָה עִם הַהִסְטוֹרְיָה הַגָּלוּתִית שֶׁלָּנוּ, לְלֹא מְלוּכָה וּלְלֹא אֶרֶץ. כְּמוֹ כֵן לֹא יְכוֹלָה הַשָּׂפָה לְהֵחָשֵׁב יְסוֹד חִיּוּנִי בְּקִיּוּמֵנוּ, כִּי עוֹד בִּימֵי קֶדֶם שִׁמְּשָׁה אֲרָמִית כִּשְׂפַת דִּיבּוּר שֶׁל הָעָם: חֲלָקִים שֶׁל הַתַּנַ"ךְ, כִּמְעַט כָּל תַּלְמוּד בַּבְלִי, הַזֹּהַר וְעוֹד, נִכְתְּבוּ בַּלָּשׁוֹן הָאֲרָמִית. בִּימֵי ר' סַעֲדְיָה גָּאוֹן וְהָרַמְבַּ"ם הָיְתָה הַשָּׂפָה הָעַרְבִית שְׂפָתָם שֶׁל רוֹב הֲמוֹנֵי הָעָם, וּלְאַחַר מִכֵּן אִידִישׁ וְשָׂפוֹת אֲחֵרוֹת. כְּמוֹ כֵן אִי אֶפְשָׁר לוֹמַר שֶׁמִּין תַּרְבּוּת אוֹ מַדָּע כְּלָלִיִּים הִבְטִיחוּ אֶת קִיּוּם אוּמָּתֵינוּ, כִּי דְבָרִים אֵלֶּה נִשְׁתַּנּוּ בְּתַכְלִית מִתְּקוּפָה לִתְקוּפָה.

נִשְׁאַר רַק דָּבָר אֶחָד, שֶׁהוּא הַצַּד הַשָּׁוֶה לְכָל הַזְּמַנִּים, כָּל הָאֲרָצוֹת וְכָל הַתְּנָאִים שֶׁבְּדִבְרֵי יָמֵינוּ

- הַתּוֹרָה וְהַמִּצְווֹת שֶׁשָּׁמְרוּ בְּנֵי יִשְׂרָאֵל בְּחַיֵּיהֶם
הַיּוֹם-יוֹמִיִּים בִּמְסִירוּת נֶפֶשׁ גְּדוֹלָה בְּיוֹתֵר.

An objective, unprejudiced survey of the long history of our people will at once bring to light the reality that our survival as a nation was not the result of material wealth or physical strength. Even during the most prosperous times under the united monarchy of King Solomon, the Jewish people, as well as its country, were materially insignificant by comparison with contemporary world empires such as Egypt, Assyria, and Babylonia.

Nor was it our active statehood or the control of our geographic homeland that secured our existence, as is evidenced from the reality that for the vast majority of our history, our people have lived in exile—without a kingdom and without a homeland.

Similarly, our Hebrew language did not play a vital role in our perpetuation, for even in biblical times, Aramaic supplanted the Holy Tongue as the spoken language, to the extent that parts of the Scripture, almost all of our Babylonian Talmud, the *Zohar*, and other key works were composed in Aramaic instead of Hebrew. Later, in the times of Rabbi Saadya Ga'on and Maimonides, most of the Jewish masses spoke Arabic, and further down the line, it was Yiddish and other languages.

It is also impossible to ascribe any common secular culture or contemporary scientific knowledge as a major preservation factor for our people, since such matters morphed radically from one era to another.

The only remaining consideration, which is the sole factor that has remained consistent throughout the ages, in all lands, and under the fullest diversity of circumstance, is the Torah and *mitzvot* that the Jews have observed in their daily life with great self-sacrifice.

The *Birds' Head Haggadah* is the oldest surviving illuminated Passover *Haggadah*, created in Germany in the early fourteenth century. Much has been written about its unusual iconography—the substitution of birds' heads for almost all the human heads in the manuscript. We know from contemporary sources (see *Tosafot*, Yoma 54a) that some Jews believed it was inappropriate to depict a human face, and this may explain why animal heads were used as a substitute. On this page, Moses receives two Tablets, and the Jews faithfully pass along the Five Books of Moses from one generation to the next. The lamb represents the application of the Torah into actual practice, expressed by the yearly celebration of the Passover ritual (which in Temple times included the preparation of the Paschal lamb). It should be noted that the Talmud states that the two Tablets were square, with flat tops; the round tops in this drawing are consistent with the unrealistic nature of this art. (Israel Museum, Jerusalem)

TEXT 11

The Lay of the Land

The Rebbe, Rabbi Menachem Mendel Schneerson,
Likutei Sichot, vol. 30, pp. 250–251

וְהַמַּעֲנֶה עַל זֶה . . . נְתִינַת אֶרֶץ יִשְׂרָאֵל לְעַם יִשְׂרָאֵל אֵינָה כְּמוֹ אֵצֶל שְׁאָר הָאֻמּוֹת לְהַבְדִּיל - אֶלָּא הִיא חֵלֶק **בַּעֲבוֹדָתָם**, לְגַלּוֹת "כֹּחַ מַעֲשָׂיו" שֶׁל הַקָּבָּ"ה.

תַּכְלִית עֲבוֹדָתָם שֶׁל בְּנֵי יִשְׂרָאֵל הִיא לַעֲשׂוֹת לוֹ יִתְבָּרֵךְ דִּירָה **בְּתַחְתּוֹנִים** דַּוְקָא, שֶׁקְּדֻשָּׁתוֹ יִתְבָּרֵךְ תִּשְׁרֶה בְּ"אַרְצִיּוּת" שֶׁל עוֹלָם הַזֶּה הַגַּשְׁמִי דַּוְקָא (שֶׁלָּכֵן רֹב מִצְוֹת הַתּוֹרָה הֵן מִצְוֹת מַעֲשִׂיּוֹת, כְּדֵי שֶׁעַל יְדֵי קִיּוּם הַתּוֹרָה וּמִצְוֹת תּוּמְשַׁךְ קְדוּשָּׁה (גַּם) בְּעִנְיָנִים הַגַּשְׁמִיִּים) . . . לָכֵן דַּוְקָא מִשּׁוּם זֶה נִיתְּנָה לוֹ אֶרֶץ יִשְׂרָאֵל, אֶרֶץ גַּשְׁמִית, שֶׁבָּהּ תְּלוּיוֹת כַּמָּה וְכַמָּה מִצְוֹת הַתּוֹרָה . . . מֵאַחַר שֶׁזֶּהוּ עִנְיַן בְּנֵי יִשְׂרָאֵל וְהַתּוֹרָה - "לִכְבּשׁ" אֶת "הָאַרְצִיּוּת" שֶׁל עוֹלָם הַזֶּה וְלַעֲשׂוֹתוֹ דִּירָה לוֹ יִתְבָּרֵךְ.

The response to this is that . . . the relationship between the Jewish people and the Land of Israel is unique. It is not comparable to the relationship between any other nation and its homeland. Rather, the Jewish land is an integral part of the Jewish people's *spiritual mission*.

The ultimate goal of the Jewish people's divine service is to turn this tangible world into a home for G-dly revelation, to the point that G-d's holiness dwells specifically in the *physical* reality of this world. For this reason, the majority of the Torah's commandments involve *physical* activities, so that the fulfillment of Torah and *mitzvot* installs sanctity into tangible materials. . . .

It was therefore critical to provide the Jews with the Land of Israel, a *physical* land, and to provide them with an abundance of *mitzvot* that can be performed exclusively with this Land. . . . For this expresses the entire goal of the Jewish people and the purpose of the Torah—to "conquer" the physical dimension of the world and transform it into a home for G-d.

Professor **Cary Nelson** explains the unique relationship between the Jewish people and the Land of Israel: **myjli.com/*antisemitism***

ISRAELI LANDSCAPE
Israel Paldi, oil on canvas, 1928.
(Israel Museum, Jerusalem)

KEY POINTS

1 Antisemitism seeks legitimacy from the most prestigious authority of any given era. At present, this authority is the pursuit of human rights. Consequently, many of today's antisemites focus overwhelmingly on Israel and accuse it of being the ultimate violator of human rights.

2 When Israel is (a) demonized, or (b) judged with a double standard, or (c) when Israel's existence is delegitimized, the challenge exposes itself as an expression of antisemitism.

3 When antisemites refrain from asserting that they seek to annihilate Jewry but merely take issue with specific Jewish beliefs or practices, claiming them to be barbaric, Jews can be tempted to join the fight against their fellow Jews, believing they are saving Jews rather than hurting them.

4 There are several arguments for why Jews need, and have a right to, Israel. Most crucial is the Torah's oft-reiterated reminder that G-d gave the Jews the Land of Israel as an eternal inheritance. The deeper our appreciation of this reality, and the more we educate the next generation about its implications, the more support we will nourish toward the Land of Israel. Such an approach

can desirably influence the wider audience, but the most vital audience is our Jewish brothers and sisters.

5. To support Torah and G-d-based reasoning, it is necessary to create an environment that cherishes the Torah and nurtures faith. It is, therefore, critical to provide a robust Jewish education to ourselves and to the next generation.

6. Jews are a nation not because of our Land but because of our Torah. Nevertheless, the Land is important to the Torah's vision for the world inasmuch as it embodies the Jewish mission on earth: to infuse physicality with holiness.

Double Standard: Settlement Activity in Occupied Territories

Israel is routinely condemned by international bodies for the existence of Jewish settlements in the Palestinian Territories. These settlements are said to be a violation of international law and an obstacle to peace. The following map shows that in recent times, prolonged occupation of a territory by a neighboring power has always been accompanied by large-scale settlement by citizens of the occupying power in the occupied territory. Yet the UN and other international bodies have never deemed any of these instances of settlement to be a violation of international law, and removal of the settlers has never been established as a necessary condition for a peaceful resolution of the conflict.

Based on Eugene Kontorovich, "Unsettled: A Global Study of Settlements in Occupied Territories," *Journal of Legal Analysis*, Volume 9, Issue 2, Winter 2017

ICON KEYS

Occupying power | Duration of conflict | Number of settlers

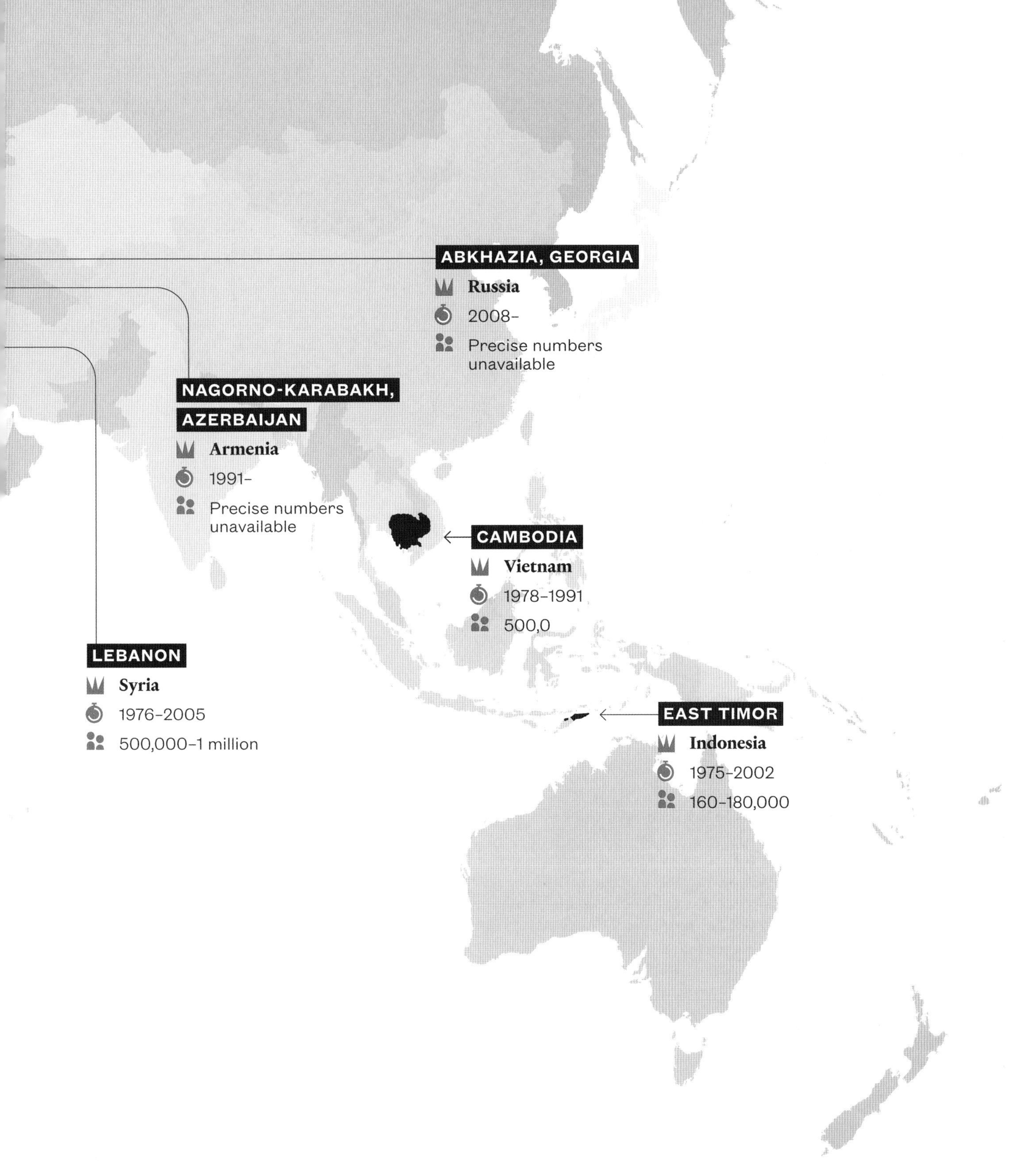
ABKHAZIA, GEORGIA
Russia
2008–
Precise numbers unavailable
NAGORNO-KARABAKH, AZERBAIJAN
Armenia
1991–
Precise numbers unavailable
CAMBODIA
Vietnam
1978–1991
500,0
LEBANON
Syria
1976–2005
500,000–1 million
EAST TIMOR
Indonesia
1975–2002
160–180,000

Working Definition of Antisemitism

The International Holocaust Remembrance Alliance (IHRA) unites governments and experts to strengthen, advance, and promote Holocaust education. In May 2016, it proposed the following "working definition of antisemitism":

"Antisemitism is a certain perception of Jews, which may be expressed as hatred toward Jews. Rhetorical and physical manifestations of antisemitism are directed toward Jewish or non-Jewish individuals and/or their property, toward Jewish community institutions and religious facilities."

The countries listed on this map have adopted or endorsed this working definition of antisemitism. The IHRA provides the following contemporary examples of antisemitism that may serve as illustrations:

Source: www.holocaustremembrance.com

- Calling for, aiding, or justifying the killing or harming of Jews in the name of a radical ideology or an extremist view of religion.
- Making mendacious, dehumanizing, demonizing, or stereotypical allegations about Jews as such or the power of Jews as collective—such as, especially but not exclusively, the myth about a world Jewish conspiracy or of Jews controlling the media, economy, government or other societal institutions.
- Accusing Jews as a people of being responsible for real or imagined wrongdoing committed by a single Jewish person or group, or even for acts committed by non-Jews.
- Denying the fact, scope, mechanisms (e.g., gas chambers) or intentionality of the genocide of the Jewish people at the hands of National Socialist Germany and its supporters and accomplices during World War II (the Holocaust).
- Accusing the Jews as a people, or Israel as a state, of inventing or exaggerating the Holocaust.
- Accusing Jewish citizens of being more loyal to Israel, or to the alleged priorities of Jews worldwide, than to the interests of their own nations.

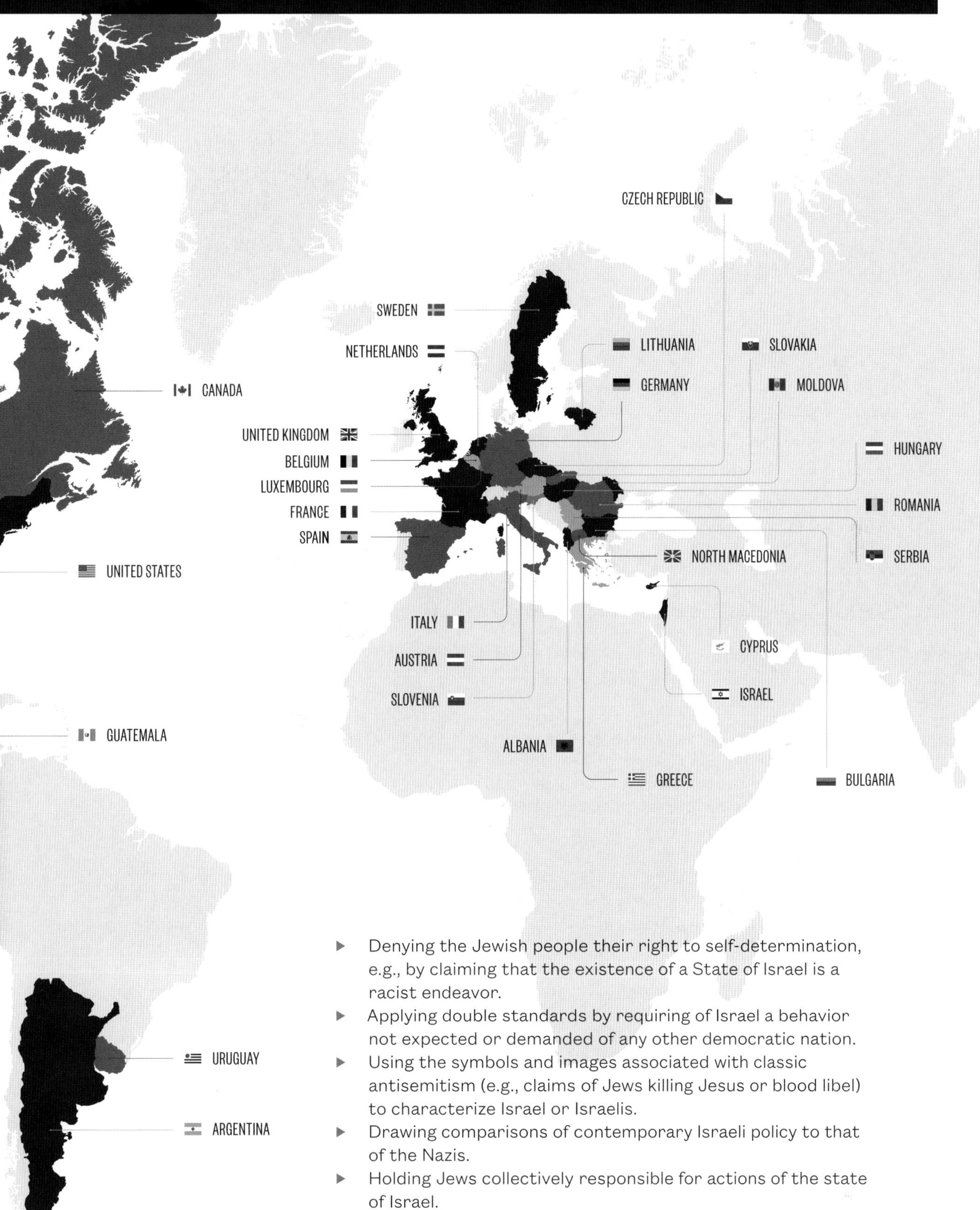

- Denying the Jewish people their right to self-determination, e.g., by claiming that the existence of a State of Israel is a racist endeavor.
- Applying double standards by requiring of Israel a behavior not expected or demanded of any other democratic nation.
- Using the symbols and images associated with classic antisemitism (e.g., claims of Jews killing Jesus or blood libel) to characterize Israel or Israelis.
- Drawing comparisons of contemporary Israeli policy to that of the Nazis.
- Holding Jews collectively responsible for actions of the state of Israel.

THE SYNAGOGUE
Hyman Bloom, oil on canvas, c. 1940. (Museum of Modern Art, Licensed by SCALA / Art Resource, New York)

CHANGE OF HEART

Psychology, neuroscience, and recent history show us that neither friend nor foe should ever be taken for granted. With a bit of subtlety and conviction, and always with trust in G-d, we find that the dark days of the past are no cause for pessimism ahead.

I. INTRODUCTION

The final chapter of *Outsmarting Antisemitism* addresses the question of responding to, approaching, and handling public figures who support policies or employ rhetoric that undermines Jews and their safety.

The question is not new. It is as old as the Jewish nation itself. One among a myriad of examples of the issue was the 1970 French Mirage saga: during the Arab War of Attrition against Israel, French President Georges Pompidou announced the sale of an entire fleet of Mirage jets to Libya, a sworn enemy of Israel, even as the French maintained an arms embargo against Israel.

Then, as now, Jews had to consider what strategy would best serve as a countermeasure.

EXERCISE 4.1

List famous living individuals who embrace opinions or have acted in ways that are harmful to Jews.

Journalism

Entertainment

Politics

Academia

TEXT 1

Mirage Jets to Libya

Henry Giniger, "France Confirms Libyans Will Get 50 Mirage Planes," *The New York Times*, January 10, 1970

After much hesitation, French officials acknowledged tonight that about 50 Mirage jet fighter planes would be sold to Libya. . . . The confirmation of the sale . . . was expected to provoke sharp protests from Israel. The Israelis suspect that the planes will sooner or later find their way to the fighting fronts. . . .

[The French Defense Ministry] reaffirmed the French embargo policy of selling no arms to the countries directly in conflict—Israel, the United Arab Republic, Jordan and Syria—and said that they were convinced that Libya sought to supply her own forces.

Israeli fears of the Libyan Mirages is based on a conviction shared by some French experts that the Libyan Air Force in its present state could not absorb such numbers of a highly advanced plane. The fear is compounded by the aggressive stance taken toward Israel by the new revolutionary military regime, which has been in power in Libya since early September. . . .

The plane sold to Libya is believed to be the Mirage III, the same type as the 50 built for Israel but placed under embargo in 1967. The Israelis are expected to find particularly galling the fact that they have been denied about the same number of planes now made available to a hostile Arab country.

EXERCISE 4.2

What might be the best strategy for dealing with a public figure who takes an unfavorable position toward us? List three significant dos and don'ts.

Dos

Don'ts

II. JACOB'S MODEL

Throughout history, Jews have had to carefully consider how to best deal with their enemies. Our patriarch Jacob crafted a multipronged approach to the mortal hatred of Esau. Nevertheless, his preference was to win him over, at least temporarily, via gift giving, warm words, and creating a favorable impression. He was successful; Esau dropped his plan of attack and ran to kiss him.

This model was employed by Jews of each era. One Talmudic sage would read Jacob's story in the Torah before each meeting with Roman officials. Another sage, who had insisted that Roman Jew-hatred was irremediable, tried to win concessions from them nevertheless. So-called "court Jews" often engaged non-Jewish rulers and sought to sway them for the benefit of the Jewish community. Sometimes they were unsuccessful, as in the 1492 Spanish Expulsion, while other cases met with resounding success, such as the sixteenth-century saga of Yosef of Rosheim.

The *Sarajevo Haggadah* was copied and illuminated on vellum in Barcelona, in approximately 1350 CE. It opens with thirty-four pages of illustrations that depict biblical scenes, including this one, about the lives of Jacob and Esau. The right side presents Rebecca giving birth to Jacob and Esau; the left side depicts Jacob studying Torah while Esau is out on a hunt. (National Museum of Bosnia and Herzegovina, Sarajevo)

TEXT 2

Three Steps

Midrash, *Tanchuma* (Buber), Vayishlach 6

וְהִתְקִין עַצְמוֹ לִשְׁלֹשָׁה דְבָרִים,
לִתְפִלָּה וּלְדוֹרוֹן וּלְמִלְחָמָה.

Jacob prepared himself for a three-pronged response: a prayer, a gift, and armed struggle.

TEXT 3

Fraternal Embrace

Genesis 33:4

וַיָּרָץ עֵשָׂו לִקְרָאתוֹ, וַיְחַבְּקֵהוּ,
וַיִּפֹּל עַל צַוָּארָו, וַיִּשָּׁקֵהוּ, וַיִּבְכּוּ.

Esau ran toward Jacob and embraced him,
he fell on Jacob's neck and kissed him, and they wept.

TANCHUMA

A Midrashic work bearing the name of Rabbi Tanchuma, a 4th-century Talmudic sage quoted often in this work. "Midrash" is the designation of a particular genre of rabbinic literature usually forming a running commentary on specific books of the Bible. *Tanchuma* provides textual exegeses, expounds upon the biblical narrative, and develops and illustrates moral principles. *Tanchuma* is unique in that many of its sections commence with a halachic discussion, which subsequently leads into nonhalachic teachings.

Mr. **Natan Sharansky** talks about his little Book of Psalms that helped him survive Soviet prison: **myjli.com/*antisemitism***

TEXT 4

Deciphering the Heart

Sifrei, Bamidbar 69

"וַיִּשָּׁקֵהוּ" - נָקוּד עָלָיו, שֶׁלֹּא נְשָׁקוֹ בְּכָל לִבּוֹ.

רַבִּי שִׁמְעוֹן בֶּן יוֹחַאי אוֹמֵר: הֲלָכָה בְּיָדוּעַ שֶׁעֵשָׂו שׂוֹנֵא לְיַעֲקֹב, אֶלָּא נֶהֶפְכוּ רַחֲמָיו בְּאוֹתָהּ שָׁעָה וּנְשָׁקוֹ בְּכָל לִבּוֹ.

The Torah features dots over the words, "And kissed him." This is because Esau did not kiss Jacob wholeheartedly.

Rabbi Shimon ben Yocha'i said: "It is an established fact that Esau hates Jacob. Nevertheless, his compassion was moved at that time and he kissed him wholeheartedly."

SIFREI

An early rabbinic Midrash on the biblical books of Numbers and Deuteronomy. *Sifrei* focuses mostly on matters of law, as opposed to narratives and moral principles. According to Maimonides, this halachic Midrash was authored by Rav, a 3rd-century Babylonian Talmudic sage.

QUESTION

What lessons does this episode provide the Jewish people in terms of dealing with their foes?

TEXT 5

Diplomatic Planning

Nachmanides, Genesis 33:15

אָמְרוּ (בְּרֵאשִׁית רַבָּה עח, טו) רַבִּי יַנַּאי כַּד הֲוָה סָלִיק לְמַלְכוּתָא הֲוָה מִסְתַּכֵּל בְּהָדָא פָּרָשָׁתָא . . . מִפְּנֵי שֶׁהָיְתָה קַבָּלָה בְּיָדָם שֶׁזוֹ פָּרָשַׁת גָלוּת, כְּשֶׁהָיָה בָּא בְּרוֹמָה בַּחֲצַר מַלְכֵי אֱדוֹם עַל עִסְקֵי הַצִּבּוּר הָיָה מִסְתַּכֵּל בְּפָרָשָׁה זוּ לָלֶכֶת אַחֲרֵי עֲצַת הַזָּקֵן הֶחָכָם, כִּי מִמֶּנּוּ יִרְאוּ הַדּוֹרוֹת וְכֵן יַעֲשׂוּ.

The Midrash relates (*BEREISHIT RABAH* 78:15) that when Rabbi Yanai would set out for a meeting with the Roman government, he would first read this passage in the Torah regarding Jacob and Esau. . . . The sages had a tradition that this passage was a guide for our exile. Therefore, when Rabbi Yanai would visit the rulers of Rome for communal issues, he would consult this passage to follow the advice of the wise Jacob. It is indeed appropriate for all generations to study his approach and to adopt it in actual practice.

RABBI MOSHE BEN NACHMAN (NACHMANIDES, RAMBAN)
1194–1270

Scholar, philosopher, author, and physician. Nachmanides was born in Spain and served as leader of Iberian Jewry. In 1263, he was summoned by King James of Aragon to a public disputation with Pablo Cristiani, a Jewish apostate. Though Nachmanides was the clear victor of the debate, he had to flee Spain because of the resulting persecution. He moved to Israel and helped reestablish communal life in Jerusalem. He authored a classic commentary on the Pentateuch and a commentary on the Talmud.

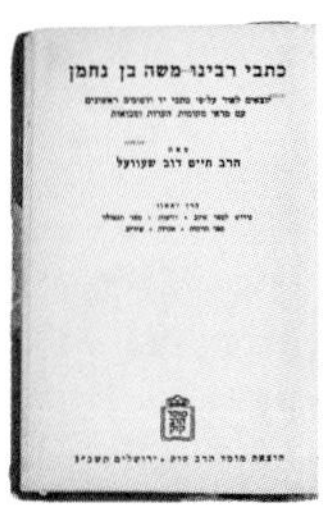

TEXT 6

Rabbi Shimon to Rome

Talmud, Me'ilah 17a

שֶׁפַּעַם אַחַת גָּזְרָה הַמַּלְכוּת גְּזֵרָה שֶׁלֹּא יִשְׁמְרוּ אֶת הַשַּׁבָּת וְשֶׁלֹּא יָמוּלוּ אֶת בְּנֵיהֶם וְשֶׁיִּבְעֲלוּ אֶת נִדּוֹת . . .

אָמְרוּ מִי יֵלֵךְ וִיבַטֵּל הַגְּזֵרוֹת? יֵלֵךְ רַבִּי שִׁמְעוֹן בֶּן יוֹחַאי שֶׁהוּא מְלוּמָּד בְּנִסִּים . . .

The Roman government once issued a decree that Jews may not observe Shabbat, circumcision, and family purity. . . .

The Jews said to themselves, "Who should go to Rome to solicit annulment of the decree? Let Rabbi Shimon ben Yocha'i go, for he is experienced in miracles."

BABYLONIAN TALMUD

A literary work of monumental proportions that draws upon the legal, spiritual, intellectual, ethical, and historical traditions of Judaism. The 37 tractates of the Babylonian Talmud contain the teachings of the Jewish sages from the period after the destruction of the 2nd Temple through the 5th century CE. It has served as the primary vehicle for the transmission of the Oral Law and the education of Jews over the centuries; it is the entry point for all subsequent legal, ethical, and theological Jewish scholarship.

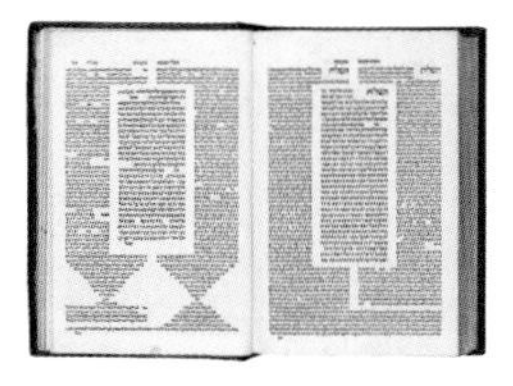

A fourteenth-century miniature from the *Alexander Romance* depicting the Jews offering gold and silver to Alexander the Great. The scene is depicted in Byzantine fashion: Alexander is depicted as a Byzantine emperor and his troops are depicted as Byzantine-Greek soldiers of the fourteenth century. The Jews are shown wearing distinctive ceremonial robes and small caps.

FIGURE 4.1

Jewish Advocates in Central Europe: 1500–1800

Based on Sir Martin Gilbert, *The Atlas of Jewish History* (New York: William Morrow and Company, 1993), pp. 54–55

Joseph of Rosheim

Vienna (1480-1554)

Jewish advocate at the courts of Maximilian I and Charles V. A rabbinic scholar and kabbalist, he is primarily known as the skillful intermediary on behalf of German and Polish Jews. One of his famous achievements was saving the Talmud from the flames in 1510.

Jacob Bassevi

Prague (1580-1634)

Rendered financial assistance to emperors Rudolph II, Matthias, and Ferdinand II, and was made a nobleman by the latter. Due to his efforts, the Jewish quarter in Prague was protected by a military guard at the beginning of the Thirty Years' War.

Samuel Oppenheimer

Heidelberg (1630-1703)

Jewish banker who enjoyed the favor of Emperor Leopold I. When Johann Eisenmenger published an antisemitic work, Oppenheimer took steps to suppress it, spending large sums of money to influence the royal court and the Jesuits.

Leffman Behrends

Hanover (1630-1714)

Jewish financial agent of the dukes and princes of Hanover. In 1673, he acquired the right for Jews to open a cemetery in Hanover-Neustadt.

Samson Wertheimer

Worms (1648-1724)

Chief rabbi of Hungary and Moravia, court Jew for Austrian Emperor Leopold I. When Eisenmenger published his antisemitic work, Wertheimer petitioned Emperor Leopold. The 2000 copies of the book were confiscated and its sale was forbidden.

Joseph Süss Oppenheimer

Württemberg (1698-1738)

Confidant of Prince Carl, the Duke of Württemberg. One of the most famous court Jews, he was executed publicly on charges of stealing state funds. He was offered a pardon if he would convert to Christianity, but he chose to die as a Jew.

TEXT 7

A Court Jew

Rabbi Yosef of Rosheim, Memoirs, no. 16, in *Revue des Études Juives* (Paris: Société des Études Juives, 1888), pp. 90–91

בִּשְׁנַת רצ"א לִפְרָט קָטָן, חָזְרוּ הַמְקַטְרְגִים לִדְלֹק וְלִרְדֹּף אַחַר הַקֵּסָר בְּאֲדוֹנ', בְּרַאבַּאנְט, וְלַאנְדְרָא, אֶרֶץ אֲשֶׁר לֹא זָרוּעַ שָׁמָּה אִישׁ יוּדִי. וְנִתְעוֹרַרְתִּי מֵרַבִּים לִרְכֹּב בְּאוֹתָן מְדִינוֹת כְּדֵי לַעֲמֹד מִנֶּגֶד בְּסִיַּעְתָּא דִשְׁמַיָּא. וְהָיִיתִי בַּחֲצַר הַקֵּסָר יָרוּם הוֹדוֹ מֵרֹאשׁ חֹדֶשׁ אֲדָר עַד רֹאשׁ חֹדֶשׁ סִיוָן רצ"א בְּעִסְקֵי רַבִּים. וְאַף שֶׁבָּא הַסַרְדָאט שֶׁקּוֹרִין רוֹטְרוֹיִט לְבָלְעֵנִי חַיִּים עַד שַׁעֲרֵי מָוֶת, מִכָּל מָקוֹם, לְגֹדֶל חַסְדֵי הַמָּקוֹם שָׁלַח לְפָנַי מַלְאָכוֹ וְהִצִּלַנִי מִיָּדוֹ וּמִיַּד כָּל הָעוֹרְבִים. וּבְאוֹתָן הַיָּמִים בָּאתִי לִפְנַי וְלִפְנִים בְּחַדְרוֹ שֶׁל הַקֵּסָר לְדַבֵּר עִמּוֹ כְּפִי צָרְכִּי וְהֵשִׁיב לִי רַכּוֹת. וּבֵין כָּךְ בֶּהֱיוֹתִי פָּנוּי וּמִתְבּוֹדֵד בְּחַדְרִי, חִבַּרְתִּי הַחִבּוּר שֶׁנִּקְרָא "דֶּרֶךְ הַקֹּדֶשׁ".

In 1531, the denouncers once again hounded the emperor [Charles V] while he was in Belgium and Holland, lands uninhabited by Jews. Many requested that I travel to those lands to oppose the accusers, with the help of G-d. I was at the court of the exalted emperor for four months, from the first of Adar until the first of Sivan, pursuing the interests of the Jewish communities.

Although Rothroyt attempted to swallow me alive and to bring about my demise, G-d in His great mercy sent His messenger and saved me from his hands and from all those who sought to harm me.

RABBI YOSEF OF ROSHEIM, 1480–1554

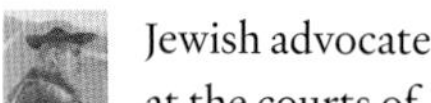

Jewish advocate at the courts of Maximilian I and Charles V. Rabbi Rosheim was a scholar and kabbalist, but he is primarily known as the skillful intermediary on behalf of German and Polish Jews. One of his famous achievements was saving the Talmud from the flames in 1510. He wrote several religious and ethical works, and his brief memoir was published in 1888.

At that time, I had an audience with the emperor in his private chamber. I spoke to him for as long as I needed, and he responded sympathetically.

During this period, when I had free time and was secluded in my room, I authored a book, entitled *The Sanctified Path*.

PROROGA D'EDITTO

IL CARDINALE SPADA LEGATO.

COntinuando la Santità di Nostro Signore gli atti della sua somma clemenza à beneficio, e sollieuo de' Popoli, s'è degnata di prorogare il termine à poter riscuotere gl'impresti, e pegni fatti alli Banchi delli Hebrei ad altri due mesi, & hauendo perciò fatto spedire il qui sotto Editto, ordiniamo, e commandiamo sia publicato, affisso, e puntualmente osseruato anche in questa nostra Legatione, acciò possi ciascuno godere gli effetti delle gratie beneficentissime di Sua Beatitudine. Dat. in Pesaro nel Palazzo Apostolico della nostra Residenza questo dì 17. Maggio 1684.

F. Card. Spada Legato.

PALVZZO del Titolo di S. Grisogono Prete Cardinal Altieri della S. R. C. Camerlengo.

ESSENDOSI per ordine preciso di Nostro Signore, ed in vigore di special Chirografo della Santità Sua segnato li 10. di Nouembre prossimo passato riuocata, & abolita tanto ogni tolleranza, & vsura, quanto l'vso di esse a gli Ebrei in qualsiuoglia luogo dello Stato Ecclesiastico, anche nelle Città di Ferrara, & Ancona dimoranti, e qualunque priuilegio conceduto a' loro Banchi, con espressa prohibitione a' medesimi di tener più Banco da far impresti [illegible] sotto vsure, [illegible] dar denari di qualsiuoglia, ancorche minima somma, ne à Christiani, ne ad altri Ebrei, ne con pegni, ne senza, come più amplamente si contiene nel sudetto Chirografo, & Editto in vigore di detto Chirografo da Noi fatto publicare in data delli 19. di Nouembre parimente prossimo passato, alli quali vogliamo che in tutto, e per tutto s'habbi relatione.

Ed essendosi tanto nel sudetto Chirografo, quanto nell'Editto già detto respettiuamente ordinato, che rispetto all'impresti già fatti, si douessero quelli andar vendendo secondo che fossero terminati i diciotto mesi dal giorno dell'impressanza, e doppo quattro mesi dalla publicatione dell'Editto medesimo, anche gli altri benche non terminati li detti mesi diciotto, di maniera che doppo i detti mesi non douessero più correre ne vsure, ne interessi.

Et essendo stato fatto ricorso da alcuni particolari della Città di Ancona alla Santità di Nostro Signore non hauer loro potuto in questo termine riscuotere i loro pegni, e perciò per indennità di quelli hauendoci ordinato, che si proroghi non solo in detta Città di Ancona, mà ancora di Ferrara, Sinigaglia, Pesaro, & ogni altro luogo dello Stato Ecclesiastico il tempo à poter riscuotere per altri due mesi prossimi dalli 20. del corrente mese di Maggio.

Per tanto Noi d'ordine della Santità Sua datoci à bocca, e per l'autorità del nostro offitio di Camerlengato proroghiamo il termine à poter riscuotere gl'impresti, e pegni sudetti ad altri due mesi prossimi, che sarà à tutto li 20. di Luglio à venire del corrente anno 1684. per il qual termine gli Ebrei sudetti dimoranti come sopra non potranno, ne douranno però in modo alcuno prendere, ne riscuotere vsure, & interessi per i sudetti pegni, mà quelli andar vendendo secondo i Capitoli, e modi praticati sin'hora, senza farsi alcuna rinouatione di essi, sotto le pene ad arbitrio di Sua Santità.

Volendo, e decretando, che il presente Editto affisso, e publicato ne i luoghi soliti di questa Città di Roma, e respettiuamente delle Città, Terre, e Luoghi dello Stato Ecclesiastico, ne' quali i detti Ebrei hanno dimorato, e dimoranò di presente, astringa ciascuno all'inuiolabile osseruanza del contenuto in esso, come se à ciascuno di loro fosse stato personalmente intimato. Dato in Roma nella Camera Apostolica questo di 15. Maggio 1684.

P. Card. Altieri Cam.

M. A. Zacharia Aud.

S. Pilastri Comm. Gen.

Domenico Liberati Segr. e Canc. della R. C. A.

In ROMA, & in PESARO, Nella Stamparia della Reuerenda Camera Apostolica. MDCLXXXIV.

EDICT PROHIBITING THE JEWS FROM LENDING AND CHANGING MONEY
May 17, 1684, Ancona, Italy. (Katz Ehrenthal Collection, United States Holocaust Memorial Museum, Washington, D.C.)

Historian **Deborah Lipstadt** discusses the role of the "court Jew" during the middle ages: **myjli.com/*antisemitism***

FIGURE 4.2

Expulsion of the Jews from Spain, 1492

Emilio Sala Francés, oil on canvas, 1889. (Museo del Prado, Madrid)

Religious symbols have been removed from this painting.

III. THE SCIENCE OF HATE

As documented above, it has been assumed throughout Jewish history—from our ancient patriarch Jacob, and at least until the early modern period—that harm to Jews could be deflected by appealing to the sentiments of those who hated them. However, this approach may seem illogical. How could anyone expect to gain something from appealing to an antisemite?

An explanation appears to have been provided by modern neuroscientific research. In his book, *Incognito: The Secret Lives of the Brain,* David Eagleman analyzes the case of actor Mel Gibson, who offered an antisemitic screed on June 28, 2006, proclaiming that "Jews are responsible for all the wars in the world!" But Gibson then apologized, saying, "There is no excuse, nor should there be any tolerance, for anyone who thinks or expresses any kind of antisemitic remark."

Rabbi Menasheh ben Israel (1604–1657) petitions Oliver Cromwell in 1655 for the readmittance of the Jews to England. The Jews had been expelled from England in 1290. (*Hutchinson's History of the Nations*, 1915)

TEXT 8A

Cognitive Diversity

David Eagleman, *Incognito: The Secret Lives of the Brain* (New York: Vintage Books, 2011), pp. 107–108, 148–149

Brains are like representative democracies. They are built of multiple, overlapping experts who weigh in and compete over different choices. . . . There is an ongoing conversation among the different factions in your brain, each competing to control the single output channel of your behavior. . . . When the hostess at a party offers chocolate cake, you find yourself on the horns of a dilemma: some parts of your brain have evolved to crave the rich energy source of the sugar, and other parts care about the negative consequences, such as the health of your heart. . . . Part of you wants the cake and part of you tries to muster the fortitude to forgo it. The final vote of the parliament determines which party controls your action—that is, whether you put your hand up or out. . . .

As the French essayist Michel de Montaigne put it, "There is as much difference between us and ourselves as there is between us and others."

DAVID EAGLEMAN
1971–

Neuroscientist and author. Born in New Mexico, David Eagleman received his PhD in neuroscience from Baylor College of Medicine. He teaches neuroscience at Stanford University and has written popular fiction and nonfiction books. Eagleman's work focuses on brain plasticity, time perceptions, and the nexus of neuroscience and law.

TEXT 8B

Team of Rivals

David Eagleman, ibid., p. 149

Returning to Mel Gibson and his drunken tirade, we can ask whether there is such a thing as "true" colors. We have seen that behavior is the outcome of the battle among internal systems. To be clear, I'm not defending Gibson's despicable behavior, but I am saying that a team-of-rivals brain can naturally harbor both racist and nonracist feelings. Alcohol is not a truth serum. Instead, it tends to tip the battle toward the short-term, unreflective faction—which has no more or less claim than any other faction to be the "true" one.

Religious symbols have been removed from this painting.

A fourteenth-century miniature of Emperor Heinrich VII's trip to Rome in 1312, where he was coronated as Holy Roman Emperor, whereupon he confirmed the rights of the Roman Jews, depicted on the right. This drawing is presented in the *Codex Balduini Trevirensis*, an illustrated chronicle made ca. 1340 for Baldwin of Luxembourg, the brother of Heinrich VII. (State Archive of Rhineland-Palatinate, Koblenz, Germany)

IV. THE MODERN ERA

Our ancestors had little choice: they could only appeal with words and gifts to win over hearts and minds. Today's scene has drastically improved: Jews enjoy previously unimaginable freedom of speech and protest, to the point that it is tempting to disparage the "court Jew" approach in favor of all-out war against those who oppose important Jewish causes, through labeling them as antisemitic and undermining their public support.

Nevertheless, the Lubavitcher Rebbe argued that the head-on approach is counterproductive and that we should maintain the timeless method of seeking to influence hearts and minds, reaching out to those we consider less than friendly to our cause. The Rebbe expressed these sentiments while discussing the cases of French President Georges Pompidou (1970) and U.S. Senator Jesse Helms (1984).

Emil Flohri, Chromolithograph, c. 1904
A Russian Jew carries a large bundle labeled "Oppression" on his back. Hanging from the bundle are weights labeled "Autocracy," "Robbery," "Cruelty," "Assassination," "Deception," and "Murder." In the background, on the right, a Jewish community burns, and in the upper left corner, American President Theodore Roosevelt (1858–1919) speaks to the Emperor of Russia, Nicholas II (1868–1918): "Stop your cruel oppression of the Jews. Now that you have peace without, why not remove his burden and have peace within your borders?" (Goldstein Foundation Collection—Prints and Drawings, U.S. Library of Congress, Washington, D.C.)

TEXT 9

An Angry President

Homer Bigart, "Jews Affronted,"
The New York Times, March 3, 1970

President Nixon made a hurried trip to New York yesterday to apologize to President Pompidou, who was angered by what he termed insults to himself and his wife during pro-Israeli demonstrations touched off by his state visit to the United States. . . . The French President had been angered by a jostling that members of his party received from demonstrators in Chicago, whose actions were marked by boos and angry cries, and by what he viewed as acceptance of such hostile acts by the Chicago police.

During a visit from French president Georges Pompidou, Jews protest against his government's decision to sell mirage jets to Libya. Tuesday, February 24, 1970. (Associated Press)

TEXT 10A

At What Cost?

The Rebbe, Rabbi Menachem Mendel Schneerson, *Torat Menachem* 5730:2 (59), pp. 395–396

יָצְאוּ לָרְחוֹב וְצָעֲקוּ וְהִפְגִּינוּ נֶגֶד צָרְפַת וְעַל יְדֵי זֶה הִכְעִיסוּ אוֹתָם. וּבְכָךְ גָּרְמוּ לְבַטֵּל אֶת הַהַשְׁפָּעָה שֶׁהָיְתָה לִיהוּדֵי צָרְפַת, שֶׁהָיוּ יְכוֹלִים לַעֲשׂוֹת מַשֶּׁהוּ כְּדֵי לִמְנֹעַ, וְעַל כָּל פָּנִים לְהַקְטִין, אֶת הַסִּיּוּעַ שֶׁל צָרְפַת לָעַרְבִים . . . הַהַסְבָּרָה שֶׁלָּהֶם הָיְתָה - שֶׁצְּרִיכִים לְהַרְאוֹת שֶׁאָמֵרִיקָא הִיא מְדִינָה דֵּמוֹקְרָטִית וִיהוּדִים אֵינָם פַּחְדָנִים.

וּבְכֵן זֶה אָמְנָם דָּבָר יָפֶה מְאוֹד, אֲבָל רַק כַּאֲשֶׁר לֹא נִמְצָאִים בְּמַצָּב שֶׁל סַכָּנָה . . . אֲבָל בְּשָׁעָה שֶׁיֵּשׁ חֲשָׁשׁ מִמִּשְׁלוֹחַ נֶשֶׁק לְלוּב (עֶשְׂרוֹת וְעַד לְ-101 אֲוִירוֹנִים), יֵשׁ לְפָנֶיךָ שְׁתֵּי בְּרֵרוֹת. אוֹ לַעֲסֹק בְּהַפְגָּנוֹת, אוֹ לַעֲשׂוֹת כָּל הַתָּלוּי בְּךָ לְעַכֵּב אֶת מִשְׁלוֹחַ הַנֶּשֶׁק לְלוּב, וְעַל כָּל פָּנִים לִפְעֹל שֶׁיִּדְחוּ אוֹתוֹ לְעוֹד ג' שָׁנִים, אוֹ לְהַקְטִין הַמִּסְפָּר אֲוִירוֹנִים . . . אוֹ שֶׁיִּשְׁלְחוּ מְקֻלְקָלִים בִּמְקוֹם טוֹבִים. פְּעֻלּוֹת שֶׁהָיוּ צְרִיכִים וִיכוֹלִים לַעֲשׂוֹת בַּחֲשַׁאי. וְהָא רְאָיָה שֶׁבֶּעָבָר עָשׂוּ וּפָעֲלוּ כַּמָּה עִנְיָנִים.

The public protests against the president of France angered French officials. This blocked any lobbying efforts that French Jews might have been able to make to prevent, or at least reduce, French assistance to Arab countries that are hostile to Israel. . . .

The stated reason for these protests was to demonstrate that America is a democratic country

RABBI MENACHEM MENDEL SCHNEERSON 1902–1994

The towering Jewish leader of the 20th century, known as "the Lubavitcher Rebbe," or simply as "the Rebbe." Born in southern Ukraine, the Rebbe escaped Nazi-occupied Europe, arriving in the U.S. in June 1941. The Rebbe inspired and guided the revival of traditional Judaism after the European devastation, impacting virtually every Jewish community the world over. The Rebbe often emphasized that the performance of just one additional good deed could usher in the era of Mashiach. The Rebbe's scholarly talks and writings have been printed in more than 200 volumes.

and that American Jews are not cowardly. This is a worthwhile objective—when Jewish lives are not at risk. . . . However, when Jews are threatened with the sale of many military jets to Libya, we have two options. We can organize public protests. Or we can make every effort to either prevent or postpone the sale, reduce the number of jets sold, . . . or to at least prevail upon the French to send less effective planes. Such aims can only be achieved through quiet diplomacy. The proof is that agreements of this nature have been reached in the past.

The sixth rebbe of Chabad, Rabbi Yosef Yitschak Schneersohn (1880–1950), with his son in law, Rabbi Shmaryahu Gurary (1897–1989), on the steps of the White House, July 10, 1930, upon their meeting with President Herbert Hoover to discuss the plight of Russian Jewry.

TEXT 10B

Quiet Diplomacy Works

The Rebbe, Rabbi Menachem Mendel Schneerson,
Torat Menachem 5731:2 (63), pp. 142–143

הָיָה סִפּוּר עִם פּוֹמְפִּידְאוּ, שֶׁבִּהְיוֹתוֹ כָּאן עָרְכוּ נֶגְדּוֹ
הַפְגָּנוֹת, וְכוּ', כֵּיוָן שֶׁחָשְׁבוּ שֶׁצָּרְפַת תִּתְיָרֵא מִזֶּה. וּמָה
קָרָה בְּפֹעַל? תְּמוּרַת זֶה שֶׁבִּתְחִלָּה הִסְכִּים לִמְכֹּר כְּלֵי נֶשֶׁק
לְאֶרֶץ יִשְׂרָאֵל, לַמְרוֹת הָאֶמְבַּרְגוֹ - עַכְשָׁו כְּבָר אֶפְשָׁר
לְסַפֵּר שֶׁלַּמְרוֹת הָאֶמְבַּרְגוֹ הִסְכִּים נְשִׂיא צָרְפַת לִמְכֹּר
לְאֶרֶץ יִשְׂרָאֵל כְּלֵי נֶשֶׁק קְטַנִּים שֶׁאֶפְשָׁר לְמָכְרָם לְלֹא
פִּרְסוּם . . . הִנֵּה בִּגְלַל הַהַפְגָּנוֹת נֶגְדּוֹ לֹא הִרְשָׁה לִמְכֹּר
יוֹתֵר . . . וּלְאַחַר שֶׁעָבַר מֶשֶׁךְ זְמַן וְהִפְסִיקוּ לְגַנּוֹתוֹ, הִתְחִילוּ
שׁוּב לְהִתְעַסֵּק אִתּוֹ בַּחֲשַׁאי, וְאָז חָזַר לִמְכֹּר כְּלֵי נֶשֶׁק
קְטַנִּים, וְכֵן פָּעַל לְהוֹצִיא שְׁלוֹשׁ מֵאוֹת יְהוּדִים מֵאֶרֶץ
מִצְרַיִם - לְלֹא הַפְגָּנוֹת, וּלְלֹא פִּרְסוּם, וְכוּ', וְהוֹרוּ לָעִתּוֹנִים
לֹא לִכְתֹּב עַל זֶה (וְרַק מֵעִתּוֹנֵי הַגּוֹיִים יוֹדְעִים עַל זֶה).

מָה הַסִּבָּה לְכָךְ? וּבְכֵן: זוֹהִי הַהוֹכָחָה שֶׁהַדֶּרֶךְ הַיְחִידָה
לִפְעֹל עַל שׂוֹנְאֵי יִשְׂרָאֵל הִיא לֹא עַל יְדֵי זֶה שֶׁבָּאִים כָּל
יוֹם וְצוֹעֲקִים: אַתָּה שׂוֹנֵא יִשְׂרָאֵל, אַתָּה גַּזְלָן וְרוֹצֵחַ וְכוּ',
אֶלָּא מְדַבְּרִים אִתָּם בְּדֶרֶךְ דִּיפְּלוֹמָטִית. הוּא יוֹדֵעַ אָמְנָם
מָה חוֹשְׁבִים עָלָיו, אֲבָל הוּא בֶּן אָדָם וּמִתְנַהֵג כְּבֶן אָדָם.

When Mr. Pompidou visited the United States, there were mass protests against him intended to intimidate France. This effort backfired. It can now be said that despite the French embargo against selling arms to belligerents in the Middle East, the

French president had allowed the sale of small arms and light weapons to Israel, items that can be sold without attracting publicity. However, as a result of the demonstrations, the approval for such sales was withdrawn. . . . After some time, when he was no longer being disparaged, he resumed dealing with Jews behind closed doors and reinstituted the small arms sales. He also arranged for three hundred Jews to be able to leave Egypt. All of this was accomplished without demonstrations and without publicity. The Jewish media was warned against disclosing any of this, and we only know of this from the non-Jewish press.

The conclusion we must draw from this case is that we do not influence antisemites by constantly yelling at them, "You are an antisemite! You are a thief! You are a murderer!" Rather, engage them in diplomatic conversation. Although such individuals are well aware of what we think about them, they are nevertheless human beings and wish to behave like human beings.

TEXT 11

Subject to Change

The Rebbe, Rabbi Menachem Mendel Schneerson, Correspondence, 1984, www.chabad.org

I trust you will agree that in regard to persons of influence, whether in Washington or elsewhere, the first objective should be to persuade and encourage such a person to use his influence in a positive way in behalf of any and all good causes which are important to us. We should welcome every public appearance which lends public support to the cause, especially when there is a likelihood that it may be the forerunner of similar pronouncements in the future. . . .

My experience with such people—though I have never personally met the said person—has convinced me that politicians are generally motivated more by expediency than by conviction. In other words, their public pronouncements on various issues do not stem from categorical principles or religious imperatives. Hence, most of them, if not all, are subject to change in their positions, depending on time, place, and other factors.

I believe, therefore, that the proper approach to such persons by Jewish leaders should not be rigid. As a rule, it does no good to engage in a cold war, which may often turn into a hot war; nor does it serve any useful purpose to brand one as an "enemy" or an "antisemite," however tempting it is to do so even if that person vehemently denies it. It can only be counterproductive. On the contrary, ways and means should be found to persuade such a person to take a favorable stance, at least publicly. We haven't too many friends, and attaching labels, etc. will not gain us any.

Instances abound where the approach advocated above produced good results. . . . There is surely no need to point out to you that responsible Jewish leaders consistently cultivated good public relations, indeed even cordial relations, with President Carter and his predecessors going back to President Roosevelt, regardless of their sometimes openly negative feelings towards Jews and Jewish causes.

Illuminated manuscript of Maimonides's *Mishneh Torah*, composed in Spain, ca. 1350. Presented here, alongside the laws of gossip and slander, is a drawing of the outlawed behavior. (The National Library of Israel, Jerusalem)

V. COURSE CONCLUSION

As this course draws to a close, we briefly review the key points of this course. Following that, a final consideration must be weighed regarding a matter that (unlike antisemitism) is mostly within our control—interactions between us and other Jews. One of the loudest messages conveyed by the ancient Purim saga is that when Jews are united, our enemies find it more difficult to undermine us.

Chanukkah
5692
(1932)
„Juda verrecke"
die Fahne spricht —
„Juda lebt ewig!"
erwidert das Licht.

On Chanukah 1932, just one month before Hitler came to power, Rachel Posner captured an indelible image: a swastika-flying building across the street, with a Chanukah menorah in the foreground, on the window ledge of her family home in Kiel, Germany. On the back she wrote:

> *"Death to Judah," so the flag says. "Judah will live forever," so the light answers.*

(United States Holocaust Memorial Museum, Washington, D.C.)

FIGURE 4.3

Course Takeaways

We will remain calm.
We will trust in G-d and upgrade our connection with Him.
We will create natural means through which G-d can provide our security.
We will not internalize antisemitism by altering our Jewish heritage.
We will be open about our Jewish identity, benefiting Jews and fostering diversity.
We will share awareness of G-d's mission for all humanity and, thereby, help individuals avoid experiencing an inner void.
We will thank G-d for the Divine gift of the Holy Land and seek to strengthen its security and prosperity.
We will avoid labels and public shaming. Instead, we will work with whomever we can to ensure beneficial results for the Jewish people.

Dr. Tammi Benjamin discusses how to overcome the startling upturn of antisemitism on American campuses: **myjli.com/*antisemitism***

TEXT 12A

Scattered and Dispersed

Esther 3:8

וַיֹּאמֶר הָמָן לַמֶּלֶךְ אֲחַשְׁוֵרוֹשׁ יֶשְׁנוֹ עַם אֶחָד
מְפֻזָּר וּמְפֹרָד בֵּין הָעַמִּים בְּכֹל מְדִינוֹת מַלְכוּתֶךָ . . .

Haman told King Ahasuerus, "There is one nation that is scattered and dispersed among the nations, throughout all the countries of your empire. . . ."

BOOK OF ESTHER

The biblical account of the Purim story. By special request of Esther to the "Men of the Great Assembly," this book was included in the biblical canon. The Book of Esther is read from a scroll twice on the holiday of Purim, the holiday that commemorates the Jews' victory over their antisemitic enemies.

Page from the *Darmstadt Haggadah*, copied around 1430 by Yisrael ben Meir of Heidelberg. Its most lavish pages show remarkable scenes of men and women passing open books and studying together, emphasizing the communal sharing of knowledge and Jewish unity. That this message appears alongside liturgy that references the persecution of Jews may allude to the idea that study, education, and unity are keys to overcoming antisemitism. (University and State Library, Darmstadt, Germany)

TEXT 12B

Divided against Itself

Rabbi Yaakov of Lissa, *Megilat Setarim* 9:19

שֶׁאָמַר הָמָן: "יֶשְׁנוֹ עַם אֶחָד מְפֻזָּר וּמְפֹרָד", וְהַיְנוּ שֶׁהֵן מְפֹרָדִים, וְאֵין לִירֹא שֶׁאֻמָּה שְׁלֵמָה יִמְצְאוּ סִבּוֹת לְהִנָּצֵל, כִּי הָיָה בֵּינֵיהֶן פֵּרוּד, וּבִלְתִּי אֶפְשָׁרִי שֶׁיִּהְיוּ כֻּלָּם בְּעֵצָה אַחַת, וְלֹא יִשְׁמְעוּ מְאוּמָה לִגְדוֹלֵיהֶם. וְאַחַר כָּךְ, כְּשֶׁשָּׁבוּ בִּתְשׁוּבָה שְׁלֵמָה, נַעֲשָׂה אַחְדוּת בֵּינֵיהֶם וְנִקְהֲלוּ בְּעָרֵיהֶם וְחִבְּבוּ זֶה אֶת זֶה. וּלְזֶה אָנוּ עוֹשִׂין וּמִשְׁלוֹחַ מָנוֹת אִישׁ לְרֵעֵהוּ לְהוֹרוֹת שֶׁעַל יְדֵי הַחִבּוּב לַחֲבֵרוֹ בָּא הַגְּאוּלָּה.

Haman claimed, "There is one nation that is scattered and dispersed." He was referring to the fact that the Jews were *internally* divided. He argued that they would be unable to defend themselves because a discordant people cannot develop a cohesive strategy, nor would they pay heed to their leaders.

Subsequently, when the Jews repented, there was unity among them and they gathered in their cities with mutual love. We therefore send packages of food to one another on Purim to demonstrate that this mutual love is a cause of our deliverance.

RABBI YAAKOV LORBERBAUM OF LISSA 1770–1832

Rabbi and halachic authority. A scion of a distinguished line of rabbis, Rabbi Lorberbaum served as the rabbi of Lissa, Poland. He was a prolific author who wrote commentaries to many books of the Bible and works of original analysis covering all areas of Jewish law. Rabbi Lorberbaum is best known for *Chavat Daat,* about matters of ritual law, and *Netivot Hamishpat*, concerning tort law.

Rabbi Adin Even-Israel Steinsaltz provides some deeper meaning to the words "I Am a Jew": **myjli.com/*antisemitism***

KEY POINTS

1. The Torah's narrative of Jacob and Esau suggests that, by employing the right words and deeds, we can influence those we deem to be against us. Accordingly, the second-century sage Rabbi Shimon bar Yocha'i traveled to Rome to win concessions for the benefit of the Jewish community, establishing a model followed by countless others, most famously, the European "court Jews" of the early modern period.

2. Jews did not feel inferior while conducting diplomatic missions. They knew that the Jewish future depended on G-d and that their job was to generate a garment behind which G-d could conceal His blessings. A firm belief that they were in G-d's hands inspired in them a sense of pride.

3. According to modern neuroscience, brains are built of multiple parts that weigh in concerning different choices, each part competing to control the single output channel of behavior. This explains why an individual with Jewish friends can nevertheless carry out a drunken tirade against Jews. Conversely, it explains why Jews can gain assistance from unlikely sources.

4 Today, we are finally able to campaign publicly against those who oppose us. However, it is often counterproductive to publicly brand individuals as enemies or antisemites. Slow to shame and quick to engage is still an effective route.

5 We must do everything possible to condition society to bring out the best in people rather than their more sinister elements. In the sphere of education this means promoting an approach that is not restricted to acquiring information but, rather, includes proper character traits, self-discipline, and the awareness that all humans are created to actively generate goodness in their environments.

6 Living in harmony with our fellow Jews enables us to better collaborate to ward off threats and promote our interests. Jewish mysticism teaches that G-d responds positively to Jewish unity, providing overt blessings of protection and goodness.

Echoes of the Past

Lessons about Antisemitism from the Purim Story

This course references the story of Purim a number of times, deriving from its nuances essential lessons for how to outsmart antisemitism. Presented here is a summary of these findings.

THE FEAST

Ancient Persian King Ahasuerus throws a mammoth feast, and invites the exiled Jews, who are **delighted to participate.** While drunk, he executes his wife. Seeking a new queen, beautiful women are selected from across his empire.

Trust in G-d

Some Jews jettisoned Judaism to gain political favor and social acceptance. We must know that protection comes from *deepening* our bond with G-d. Human endeavors depend on G-d for success.

MORDECAI, PROUD JEW

Mordecai, leading Jewish sage and palace minister, **wears his Judaism with obvious pride**. His niece Esther is forced to join the king's beauty contest and is made queen.

Jewish pride

Stuffing our Judaism beneath the public radar weakens us. Wearing Judaism proudly in public elicits respect, strengthens all minorities, and trains society to embrace diversity.

The scenes from the Purim story presented in this section are from one of the earliest extant *Megillot* (scrolls of the biblical book of Esther), dating back to 1616, written and illustrated by Moshe ben Avraham Peshkarol in Ferrara, Italy. The scroll is written in light brown ink on the flesh side of the parchment, in square Italian-Sephardic script. It features lavish marginalia depicting Esther's story as illuminated by Midrashic sources, along with faunal and floral motifs. (National Library of Israel, Jerusalem.)

UNBOWED MORDECAI

Evil Haman becomes Grand Vizier; all must bow before him. Mordecai **refuses to bow**. Haman is enraged and seeks to kill Mordecai and **all Jews.**

Hater's self-hate

The bitterest Jew-hatred results from haters hating their *own* lack of purpose to their lives, causing resentment toward a people overflowing with purpose. Sharing the Torah's insights into the purpose of life can reduce the tension.

Uncompromised Judaism

Haman established himself as a deity to whom all must bow. Mordecai, a respected palace minister, reminds us that we must be respectful of local protocol but can never jettison Judaism for it.

HAMAN'S FINAL SOLUTION

Haman asks the king to **exterminate all Jews**. He claims they are **hazardous to pagan beliefs**, disrespect the crown, and cannot live harmoniously **even with each other**. The king eagerly consents.

Mutation

Antisemites always claim that Jews undermine the society's prized value. In ancient Persia, paganism was supreme, so Haman claimed that Judaism undermined it. In recent times, it was science. Today, it is human rights. Honest analysis reveals the dishonesty in such claims.

MORDECAI IS REASSURED

Mordecai is alerted. Seeking inspiration, he asks children to quote their Torah studies, receiving a clear message: **Do not be afraid**. Relieved, he seeks a solution and inspires the Jews to repentance.

Avoid anxiety

Avoiding panic and excessive worry is key to finding constructive solutions and enables the positivity required for success and self-perpetuation.

Echoes of the Past *continued*

ESTHER'S PLAN

Mordecai asks Esther to risk her life by **appealing to the king**. She agrees but insists that Mordecai **gather the Jews for united** prayer and fasting.

Discreet action

The Jews did not launch any form of public campaign against Haman or the king. Often, it is best to work discreetly to change minds and hearts.

Jews unite

To the extent that Haman recognized Jewish disunity as a fatal flaw, Esther recognized Jewish unity as a faithful remedy for both practical and mystical purposes.

ESTHER FASTS

Esther **fasts and prays for three days** for divine assistance in dealing with the king. The king treats her favorably; she invites him and Haman to a party—and then to another.

Source of salvation

Despite needing to look sprightly to charm the king, Esther *fasted* for three days, because her appeal was primarily to G-d. Our political and other efforts are mediums, not the *cause*, of our protection and success.

MORDECAI IS HONORED

The night after Esther's first party, Haman prepares to hang Mordecai, but the king is reminded that Mordecai once saved him from assassination. He instructs Haman to lead Mordecai in an **honor parade** instead.

Jewish pride

The Jew most famous for being unashamedly Jewish was ultimately paraded with honor through society without having to compromise.

ESTHER'S COUNTERARGUMENT

At the second party, Esther **disproves Haman's conclusions** about the Jews and **begs the king** to save her and her people.

Exemplary Jew
Esther agreed that Jews are different, arguing only with Haman's conclusion: The Jewish way makes Jews *exemplary*, not evil. The proof: the king preferred a *Jewish woman* over all the ladies of his empire as his queen. We must behave in exemplary ways and let society know that it is a *result* of our Judaism.

Haters can be reformed
Haman and the king were eager to exterminate the Jews. Esther made no attempt to appease Haman, but she did appeal to the king. We should not reject *all* haters; many can be won over if handled properly.

SALVATION AND CELEBRATION

Haman is hanged, Mordecai becomes viceroy, and the Jews are permitted armed defense. On the date slated for genocide, the Jews destroy those who try to attack them. The date is celebrated as the festival of Purim, marked by acts of **charity and food gifts.**

Harmony-fostering measures
Having tasted the dangers of disunity and the saving power of unity, the Jews adopt practical measures to increase harmony. Today, practical demonstrations of unity are essential.

MORDECAI REMAINS VIGILANT

Although the danger is over, Mordecai **chooses to remain** within the king's inner circle.

Proactive approach
Vigilance and precautionary measures are constantly necessary. We must be highly *proactive* in applying all the lessons learned from the story of Purim.

Jewish Unity as a Response to Antisemitism

It has been a longstanding Jewish internal response to antisemitism to reevaluate interrelations within the Jewish community. There are two goals to this effort: (a) a practical consideration, that a discordant community cannot develop a cohesive strategy; and (b) a mystical campaign—Torah sources repeatedly insist that G-d's presence and His blessings reside more effectively among the Jews when they are united.

The following sources span two millennia of Jewish history, with each author choosing a unique way to accentuate this message.

SECRET OF SURVIVAL

Rabbi Eliezer ben Hyrcanus | *Bereishit Rabah* 38:6

1st-2nd Centuries CE

The generation of the flood, save for a single family, was entirely annihilated. Why, then, did the generation that rebelled against G-d with the tower of Babel merit to fully survive? The former folk turned against each other and were steeped in theft. By contrast, the latter generation turned against G-d but remained unified. Despite their heresy, they survived due to the power of their unity.

INVINCIBILITY

Rabbi Chiya bar Aba | *Zohar* 1:76b

2nd-3rd Centuries CE

The people joined forces to rebel against G-d with the tower of Babel. G-d predicted their success—because they were a unified people with a single language. Their unified aspiration and personal camaraderie prevented even G-d, so to speak, from thwarting them. G-d's only recourse was to splinter them by assigning them distinct languages and scattering them throughout the world.

This teaches us the power of unity: If unity enables us to rebel against G-d, it certainly empowers us to accomplish whatever we desire when we remain loyal to G-d.

LOOSE TONGUES LOSE WARS

Rabbi Ada Bar Kahana

Jerusalem Talmud, Pe'ah 1:1

4th Century CE

King David's warriors were righteous, but they failed to avoid gossip and many fell in battle. . . . King Achav's warriors were idolatrous, but they scrupulously avoided gossip and were victorious in war.

VALUE OF PEACE

Anonymous

Tractate *Kalah Rabati* 3:1

Early Middle Ages

Each Hebrew letter bears a numeric value. The combined numeric value of the letters that form the word *shalom* (שלום), "peace," is 376. There is another Hebrew word with the identical numeric value: *she'u* (שעו), "attentiveness." Their shared value conveys a critical message: G-d remains attentive to the prayers of those who pursue peace.

DISASTROUS DISCORD

Rashi

Commentary on Daniel 11:30

1040–1105

The prophet Daniel foretold the Roman destruction of Jerusalem and razing of the Temple. He predicted that the emperor would muster the confidence to attack G-d's city and Temple only upon discovering the unwarranted hatred and murder of innocents among the Jews. The emperor would be certain that their disunity would lead them to stumble in their defenses and ensure that Rome emerged triumphant.

Jewish Unity as a Response to Antisemitism *continued*

ONE FAULT, TWO MILLENNIA

Rabbi Yeshaya Halevi Horowits | *Shenei Luchot Haberit, Shaar Ha'otiyot, Beriyot*

1565–1630

The second Temple was destroyed due to a single glaring fault: vicious, unwarranted hatred between Jews. Due to this single genre of sin, G-d's Temple was lost and we were dispersed in bitter exile. And we are not done, for it continues to plague us. How many travesties and expulsions we have suffered throughout our exile only because the fog and stench of destructive hatred burns unabated!

UNWARRANTED LOVE

Rabbi Yaakov Yitschak Halevi of Lublin

Zot Zikaron, Ekev

1745–1815

The Talmud insists that unwarranted hatred was the primary cause of the second Temple's destruction. To reverse the effect, we must reverse its cause. To end our exile and bring the Redemption, we must pursue the opposite behavior—embracing each other with unity and unwarranted love.

HALTED BY HARMONY

Rabbi Yaakov Lorberbaum of Lissa | *Megilat Setarim* 9:19

1760–1832

Haman began his proposal to annihilate all Jews by describing them as "a dispersed and divided nation." His message? Their divisiveness and fractured state made them easy prey, because a divided people cannot collaborate on defensive strategy, and even if their leaders devise sound strategy, discord prevents them from accepting directions.

However, when the Jews repented and united with mutual love, their salvation arrived. We celebrate Purim annually by sending each other food gifts to emphasize that our ancestors' harmony was the cause of their redemption.

UNITY IN EGYPT

Rabbi Moshe Alshich

Commentary on Deuteronomy 26:11

1508–1593

Jacob's family traveled to Egypt to reunite with Joseph. Once there, they were in exile, removed from the Land of Israel. Yet they flourished. It was in Egypt where a family of seventy turned into a sizable nation. The secret of this growth is alluded to in the Torah. It says (Deuteronomy 10:22), "Our ancestors descended into Egypt as seventy souls," but the word used for soul, *nefesh*, is stated here in the singular rather than the plural (*nefashot*). They were unified as one. Their mutual love enabled them to flourish even in the hostile environment of Egypt. It was only later that division crept in among them.

PARENTS' PLEASURE

Rabbi Yosef Yitschak Schneersohn

Sefer Hasichot 5700, pp. 156–157

1880–1950

I asked my father why we verbally resolve to fulfill the mitzvah to love all Jews each morning, before our prayers. He explained that parents' greatest pleasure is to witness unity and love among their children. Prayer is a request for spiritual and material needs. When we verbally resolve to love G‑d's children before beseeching Him with our requests, our Father in Heaven rejoices with deep pleasure and satisfaction—and readily grants our requests.

CRITICAL DEFENSE

The Rebbe, Rabbi Menachem Mendel Schneerson

Likutei Sichot 29, pp. 5–6

1902–1994

Many believe that training an army and bolstering defenses is the best way to protect against an enemy. The truth is that, in addition to readying defenses, we must foster unity among ourselves, because a fortress provides physical protection whereas unity invokes divine protection. In times of danger, in addition to defensive efforts, the most critical weapon in our arsenal is unity.

Acknowledgments

We are grateful to the following individuals for their contributions to this course:

Course Editors
RABBI BARUCH SHALOM DAVIDSON
RABBI MORDECHAI DINERMAN

Lesson Authors
RABBI BARUCH SHALOM DAVIDSON
RABBI LAZER GURKOW
RABBI SHMUEL SUPER

Instructor Advisory Board
RABBI ZALMAN BUKIET
RABBI SHLOMIE CHEIN
RABBI YANKIE DENBURG
RABBI LEVI FRIEDMAN
RABBI LEIBEL KUDAN
RABBI MENDEL MATUSOF
RABBI RUVI NEW
RABBI YOSEF RAICHIK
RABBI DOV SCHOCHET

Flagship Director
RABBI SHMULY KARP

Curriculum Coordinator
RIVKI MOCKIN

Flagship Administrator
NAOMI HEBER

Research
RABBI YAKOV GERSHON

Copywriter
RABBI YAAKOV PALEY

Proofreading
BINA MALKA
RACHEL MUSICANTE
YA'AKOVAH WEBER

Hebrew Punctuation
RABBI MOSHE WOLFF

Design and Layout Administrator
ROCHEL KARP

Textbook and Marketing Design
CHAYA MUSHKA KANNER
RABBI LEVI WEINGARTEN

Textbook Layout
RIVKY FIELDSTEEL
SHAYNA GROSH
RABBI ZALMAN KORF

Permissions
SHULAMIS NADLER

Publication and Distribution
RABBI LEVI GOLDSHMID
RABBI MENDEL SIROTA

Branding and Marketing
AVI WEBB

PowerPoint Presentations
CHANIE DENBURG
MUSHKA DRUK
MUSHKA GOLDFARB
BAILA GOLDSTEIN
MASHIE VOGEL

Course Videos
GETZY RASKIN
MOSHE RASKIN

Key Points Videos
RABBI MOTTI KLEIN

We are immensely grateful for the encouragement of JLI's visionary chairman, and vice-chairman of *Merkos L'Inyonei Chinuch*—Lubavitch World Headquarters, **Rabbi Moshe Kotlarsky**. Rabbi Kotlarsky has been highly instrumental in building the infrastructure for the expansion of Chabad's international network and is also the architect of scores of initiatives and services to help Chabad representatives across the globe succeed in their mission. We are blessed to have the unwavering support of JLI's principal benefactor, **Mr. George Rohr**, who is fully invested in our work, continues to be instrumental in JLI's monumental growth and expansion, and is largely responsible for the Jewish renaissance that is being spearheaded by JLI and its affiliates across the globe.

The commitment and sage direction of JLI's dedicated Executive Committee—**Rabbis Chaim Block**, **Hesh Epstein**, **Ronnie Fine**, **Yosef Gansburg**, **Shmuel Kaplan**, **Yisrael Rice**, and **Avrohom Sternberg**—and the countless hours they devote to the development of JLI are what drive the vision, growth, and tremendous success of the organization.

Finally, JLI represents an incredible partnership of more than 1,600 *shluchim* and *shluchot* in more than 1,000 locations across the globe, who contribute their time and talent to further Jewish adult education. We thank them for generously sharing feedback and making suggestions that steer JLI's development and growth. They are our most valuable critics and our most cherished contributors.

Inspired by the call of the **Lubavitcher Rebbe**, of righteous memory, it is the mandate of the Rohr JLI to provide a community of learning for all Jews throughout the world where they can participate in their precious heritage of Torah learning and experience its rewards. May this course succeed in fulfilling this sacred charge!

On behalf of the Rohr Jewish Learning Institute,

RABBI EFRAIM MINTZ
Executive Director

RABBI YISRAEL RICE
Chairman, Editorial Board

3 Tammuz, 5781

The Rohr Jewish Learning Institute

AN AFFILIATE OF MERKOS L'INYONEI CHINUCH,
THE EDUCATIONAL ARM OF THE CHABAD-LUBAVITCH MOVEMENT
832 EASTERN PARKWAY, BROOKLYN, NY 11213

PAST FLAGSHIP AUTHORS

Rabbi Yitschak M. Kagan
of blessed memory

Rabbi Zalman Abraham
Brooklyn, NY

Rabbi Berel Bell
Montreal, QC

Rabbi Nissan D. Dubov
London, UK

Rabbi Tzvi Freeman
Toronto, ON

Rabbi Eliezer Gurkow
London, ON

Rabbi Aaron Herman
Pittsburgh, PA

Rabbi Simon Jacobson
New York, NY

Rabbi Chaim D. Kagan, PhD
Monsey, NY

Rabbi Shmuel Klatzkin, PhD
Dayton, OH

Rabbi Nochum Mangel
Dayton, OH

Rabbi Moshe Miller
Chicago, IL

Rabbi Yosef Paltiel
Brooklyn, NY

Rabbi Yehuda Pink
Solihull, UK

Rabbi Yisrael Rice
S. Rafael, CA

Rabbi Eli Silberstein
Ithaca, NY

Mrs. Rivkah Slonim
Binghamton, NY

Rabbi Avrohom Sternberg
New London, CT

Rabbi Shais Taub
Cedarhurst, NY

Rabbi Shlomo Yaffe
Longmeadow, MA

ROSH CHODESH SOCIETY

Rabbi Shmuel Kaplan
CHAIRMAN

Mrs. Shaindy Jacobson
DIRECTOR

Mrs. Chana Dechter
ADMINISTRATOR

Mrs. Malky Bitton
Mrs. Shula Bryski
Mrs. Chanie Wilhelm
EDITORIAL BOARD

Mrs. Devorah Kornfeld
Mrs. Chana Lipskar
Mrs. Chana Alte Mangel
Mrs. Ahuva New
Mrs. Dinie Rapoport
Mrs. Sorah Shemtov
Mrs. Binie Tenenbaum
Mrs. Yehudis Wolvovsky
STEERING COMMITTEE

JLI TEENS

In Partnership with CTeen: Chabad Teen Network

Rabbi Chaim Block
CHAIRMAN

Rabbi Shlomie Tenenbaum
DIRECTOR

TORAH STUDIES

Rabbi Yosef Gansburg
CHAIRMAN

Rabbi Shlomie Tenenbaum
PROJECT MANAGER

Rabbi Ahrele Loschak
EDITOR

Rabbi Levi Fogelman
Rabbi Yaacov Halperin
Rabbi Nechemia Schusterman
Rabbi Ari Sollish
STEERING COMMITTEE

SINAI SCHOLARS SOCIETY

In Partnership with Chabad on Campus

Rabbi Menachem Schmidt
CHAIRMAN

Rabbi Dubi Rabinowitz
DIRECTOR

Ms. Chani Chesney
Ms. Basya Hans
Ms. Mussi Rabinowitz
Mrs. Manya Sperlin
COORDINATORS

Mrs. Devorah Zlatopolsky
ADMINISTRATOR

Rabbi Shlomie Chein
VICE PRESIDENT STUDENT ENGAGEMENT, CHABAD ON CAMPUS INTERNATIONAL

Rabbi Yossy Gordon
Rabbi Efraim Mintz
Rabbi Menachem Schmidt
Rabbi Avi Weinstein
EXECUTIVE COMMITTEE

Rabbi Levi Friedman
Rabbi Chaim Leib Hilel
Rabbi Yossi Lazaroff
Rabbi Levi Raichik
Rabbi Shmuel Tiechtel
Rabbi Shmuly Weiss
STEERING COMMITTEE

THE WELLNESS INSTITUTE

Adina Lerman
ADMINISTRATOR

Rabbi Zalman Abraham
VISION AND STRATEGIC PLANNING

Pamela Dubin
IMPACT ANALYSIS

Jeffrey Wengrofsky
ACADEMIC LIAISON

Mindy Wallach
ADMINISTRATIVE SPECIALIST

Ms. Esty Levin
Mushky Lipskier
PROJECT MANAGERS

Dina Zarchi
NETWORKING AND DEVELOPMENT

Shayna Horvath
PROJECT L'CHAIM COORDINATOR

CLINICAL ADVISORY BOARD

Sigrid Frandsen-Pechenik, PSY.D.
CLINICAL DIRECTOR

Thomas Joiner, PhD
Kammarauche Asuzu, M.D., M.H.S.
Casey Skvorc, PhD, JD
David A. Brent, M.D.
Bella Schanzer, M.D.
Madelyn S. Gould, PhD, M.P.H.
Jonathan Singer, PhD, LCSW
Darcy Wallen, LCSW, PC
Gittel Francis, LMSW
Ryan G. Beale, MA, TLLP
Lisa Jacobs, M.D., MBA
Jill Harkavy-Friedman, PhD
E. David Klonsky, PhD

JLI INTERNATIONAL

Rabbi Avrohom Sternberg
CHAIRMAN

Rabbi Dubi Rabinowitz
DIRECTOR

Rabbi Berry Piekarski
ADMINISTRATOR

Rabbi Eli Wolf
ADMINISTRATOR, JLI IN THE CIS

In Partnership with the Federation of Jewish Communities of the CIS

Rabbi Shevach Zlatopolsky
EDITOR, JLI IN THE CIS

Rabbi Nochum Schapiro
REGIONAL REPRESENTATIVE, AUSTRALIA

Rabbi Avraham Golovacheov
REGIONAL REPRESENTATIVE, GERMANY

Rabbi Shmuel Katzman
REGIONAL REPRESENTATIVE, NETHERLANDS

Rabbi Avrohom Steinmetz
REGIONAL REPRESENTATIVE, BRAZIL

Rabbi Bentzi Sudak
REGIONAL REPRESENTATIVE, UNITED KINGDOM

Rabbi Shlomo Cohen
FRENCH COORDINATOR, REGIONAL REPRESENTATIVE

NATIONAL JEWISH RETREAT

Rabbi Hesh Epstein
CHAIRMAN

Mrs. Shaina B. Mintz
DIRECTOR

Bruce Backman
HOTEL LIAISON

Rabbi Menachem Klein
PROGRAM COORDINATOR

Rabbi Shmuly Karp
Rabbi Chaim Zippel
SHLUCHIM LIAISON

Rabbi Mendel Rosenfeld
LOGISTICS COORDINATOR

Ms. Rochel Karp
Mrs. Aliza Scheinfeld
SERVICE AND SUPPORT

JLI LAND & SPIRIT

Israel Experience

Rabbi Shmuly Karp
DIRECTOR

Rabbi Levi Goldshmid
SHLUCHIM LIAISON

Mrs. Shaina B. Mintz
ADMINISTRATOR

Rabbi Yechiel Baitelman
Rabbi Dovid Flinkenstein
Rabbi Chanoch Kaplan
Rabbi Levi Klein
Rabbi Mendy Mangel
Rabbi Sholom Raichik
STEERING COMMITTEE

SHABBAT IN THE HEIGHTS

Rabbi Shmuly Karp
DIRECTOR

Mrs. Shulamis Nadler
SERVICE AND SUPPORT

Rabbi Chaim Hanoka
CHAIRMAN

Rabbi Mordechai Dinerman
Rabbi Zalman Marcus
STEERING COMMITTEE

MYSHIUR

Advanced Learning Initiative

Rabbi Shmuel Kaplan
CHAIRMAN

Rabbi Shlomie Tenenbaum
ADMINISTRATOR

TORAHCAFE.COM

ONLINE LEARNING

Rabbi Mendy Elishevitz
WEBSITE DEVELOPMENT

Moshe Levin
CONTENT MANAGER

Mendel Laine
FILMING

MACHON SHMUEL

The Sami Rohr Research Institute

Rabbi Zalman Korf
ADMINISTRATOR

Rabbi Gedalya Oberlander
Rabbi Chaim Rapoport
Rabbi Levi Yitzchak Raskin
Rabbi Chaim Schapiro
Rabbi Moshe Miller
RABBINIC ADVISORY BOARD

Rabbi Yakov Gershon
RESEARCH FELLOW

FOUNDING DEPARTMENT HEADS

Rabbi Mendel Bell
Rabbi Zalman Charytan
Rabbi Mendel Druk
Rabbi Menachem Gansburg
Rabbi Meir Hecht
Rabbi Levi Kaplan
Rabbi Yoni Katz
Rabbi Chaim Zalman Levy
Rabbi Benny Rapoport
Dr. Chana Silberstein
Rabbi Elchonon Tenenbaum
Rabbi Mendy Weg

Affiliate Directory

ALABAMA

BIRMINGHAM
Rabbi Yossi Friedman 205.970.0100

MOBILE
Rabbi Yosef Goldwasser 251.265.1213

ALASKA

ANCHORAGE
Rabbi Yosef Greenberg
Rabbi Mendy Greenberg 907.357.8770

ARIZONA

CHANDLER
Rabbi Mendy Deitsch 480.855.4333

FLAGSTAFF
Rabbi Dovie Shapiro 928.255.5756

FOUNTAIN HILLS
Rabbi Mendy Lipskier 480.776.4763

PHOENIX
Rabbi Zalman Levertov
Rabbi Yossi Friedman 602.944.2753

SCOTTSDALE
Rabbi Yossi Levertov 480.998.1410

TUCSON
Rabbi Yehuda Ceitlin 520.881.7956

CALIFORNIA

ALAMEDA
Rabbi Meir Shmotkin 510.640.2590

BEL AIR
Rabbi Chaim Mentz 310.475.5311

BURBANK
Rabbi Shmuly Kornfeld 818.954.0070

CARLSBAD
Rabbi Yeruchem Eilfort
Mrs. Nechama Eilfort 760.943.8891

CONTRA COSTA
Rabbi Dovber Berkowitz 925.937.4101

DANVILLE
Rabbi Shmuli Raitman 213.447.6694

ENCINO
Rabbi Aryeh Herzog 818.784.9986
Chapter founded by Rabbi Joshua Gordon, OBM

FOLSOM
Rabbi Yossi Grossbaum 916.608.9811

FREMONT
Rabbi Moshe Fuss 510.300.4090

GLENDALE
Rabbi Simcha Backman 818.240.2750

GRANADA HILLS
Rabbi Meir Rivkin 818.493.9250

HUNTINGTON BEACH
Rabbi Aron David Berkowitz 714.846.2285

LA JOLLA
Rabbi Baruch Shalom Ezagui 858.455.5433

LOMITA
Rabbi Eli Hecht
Rabbi Sholom Pinson 310.326.8234

LOS ANGELES
Rabbi Leibel Korf 323.660.5177

MALIBU
Rabbi Levi Cunin 310.456.6588

MARINA DEL REY
Rabbi Danny Yiftach-Hashem
Rabbi Dovid Yiftach 310.859.0770

MARVISTA
Rabbi Shimon Simpson 646.401.2354

NEWHALL
Rabbi Choni Marosov 661.254.3434

NORTHRIDGE
Rabbi Eli Rivkin 818.368.3937

OJAI

Rabbi Mordechai Nemtzov 805.613.7181

PACIFIC PALISADES

Rabbi Zushe Cunin 310.454.7783

PALO ALTO

Rabbi Menachem Landa 415.418.4768
Rabbi Yosef Levin
Rabbi Ber Rosenblatt 650.424.9800

PASADENA

Rabbi Chaim Hanoka
Rabbi Sholom Stiefel 626.539.4578

PLEASANTON

Rabbi Josh Zebberman 925.846.0700

POWAY

Rabbi Mendel Goldstein 858.208.6613
Rabbi Yehoshua Goldstein 858.842.7707

RANCHO MIRAGE

Rabbi Shimon H. Posner 760.770.7785

RANCHO PALOS VERDES

Rabbi Yitzchok Magalnic 310.544.5544

RANCHO S. FE

Rabbi Levi Raskin 858.756.7571

REDONDO BEACH

Rabbi Yossi Mintz
Rabbi Zalman Gordon 310.214.4999

RIVERSIDE

Rabbi Shmuel Fuss 951.329.2747

S. CLEMENTE

Rabbi Menachem M. Slavin 949.489.0723

S. CRUZ

Rabbi Yochanan Friedman 831.454.0101

S. DIEGO

Rabbi Zalman Carlebach 619.301.7450

S. FRANCISCO

Rebbetzin Mattie Pil 415.933.4310
Rabbi Gedalia Potash 415.648.8000
Rabbi Shlomo Zarchi 415.752.2866

S. MATEO

Rabbi Yossi Marcus 650.341.4510

S. RAFAEL

Rabbi Yisrael Rice 415.492.1666

SUNNYVALE

Rabbi Yisroel Hecht 408.720.0553

TEMECULA

Rabbi Yonason Abrams 951.234.4196

TUSTIN

Rabbi Yehoshua Eliezrie 714.508.2150

VACAVILLE

Rabbi Chaim Zaklos 707.592.5300

WEST LOS ANGELES

Rabbi Mordechai Zaetz 424.652.8742

YORBA LINDA

Rabbi Dovid Eliezrie 714.693.0770

COLORADO

ASPEN

Rabbi Mendel Mintz 970.544.3770

DENVER

Rabbi Yossi Serebryanski 303.744.9699
Rabbi Mendy Sirota 720.940.3716

FORT COLLINS

Rabbi Yerachmiel Gorelik 970.407.1613

HIGHLANDS RANCH

Rabbi Avraham Mintz 303.694.9119

VAIL

Rabbi Dovid Mintz 970.476.7887

WESTMINSTER

Rabbi Benjy Brackman 303.429.5177

CONNECTICUT

GREENWICH

Rabbi Yossi Deren
Rabbi Menachem Feldman 203.629.9059

HAMDEN

Rabbi Moshe Hecht 203.635.7268

MILFORD

Rabbi Schneur Wilhelm 203.887.7603

NEW HAVEN
Rabbi Mendy Hecht 203.589.5375

NEW LONDON
Rabbi Avrohom Sternberg 860.437.8000

STAMFORD
Rabbi Yisrael Deren
Rabbi Levi Mendelow 203.3.CHABAD

WEST HARTFORD
Rabbi Shaya Gopin 860.232.1116

DELAWARE

WILMINGTON
Rabbi Chuni Vogel 302.529.9900

DISTRICT OF COLUMBIA

WASHINGTON
Rabbi Levi Shemtov
Rabbi Yitzy Ceitlin 202.332.5600

FLORIDA

ALTAMONTE SPRINGS
Rabbi Mendy Bronstein 407.280.0535

BAL HARBOUR
Rabbi Dov Schochet 305.868.1411

BOCA RATON
Rabbi Zalman Bukiet
Rabbi Arele Gopin 561.994.6257
Rabbi Moishe Denburg 561.526.5760
Rabbi Ruvi New 561.394.9770

BOYNTON BEACH
Rabbi Yosef Yitzchok Raichik 561.732.4633

BRADENTON
Rabbi Menachem Bukiet 941.388.9656

CAPE CORAL
Rabbi Yossi Labkowski 239.963.4770

CORAL GABLES
Rabbi Avrohom Stolik 305.490.7572

CORAL SPRINGS
Rabbi Yankie Denburg 954.471.8646

CUTLER BAY
Rabbi Yossi Wolff 305.975.6680

DAVIE
Rabbi Aryeh Schwartz 954.376.9973

DELRAY BEACH
Rabbi Sholom Ber Korf 561.496.6228

FISHER ISLAND
Rabbi Efraim Brody 347.325.1913

FLEMING ISLAND
Rabbi Shmuly Feldman 904.290.1017

FORT LAUDERDALE
Rabbi Yitzchok Naparstek 954.568.1190

HALLANDALE BEACH
Rabbi Mordy Feiner 954.458.1877

HOLLYWOOD
Rabbi Leibel Kudan 954.801.3367

JUPITER
Rabbi Berel Barash 561.317.0968

KENDALL
Rabbi Yossi Harlig 305.234.5654

LAUDERHILL
Rabbi Shmuel Heidingsfeld 323.877.7703

LONGWOOD
Rabbi Yanky Majesky 407.636.5994

MARION COUNTY
Rabbi Yossi Hecht 352.330.4466

MAITLAND
Rabbi Sholom Dubov
Rabbi Levik Dubov 470.644.2500

MIAMI
Rabbi Mendy Cheruty 305.219.3353
Rabbi Yakov Fellig 305.445.5444

MIAMI BEACH
Rabbi Yisroel Frankforter 305.534.3895

N. MIAMI BEACH
Rabbi Eli Laufer 305.770.4412

ORLANDO
Rabbi Yosef Konikov 407.354.3660

ORMOND BEACH
Rabbi Asher Farkash 386.672.9300

PALM BEACH
Rabbi Zalman Levitin 561.659.3884

PALM BEACH GARDENS
Rabbi Dovid Vigler 561.624.2223

PALM HARBOR
Rabbi Pinchas Adler 727.789.0408

PEMBROKE PINES
Rabbi Mordechai Andrusier 954.874.2280

PLANTATION
Rabbi Pinchas Taylor 954.644.9177

PONTE VEDRA BEACH
Rabbi Nochum Kurinsky 904.543.9301

S. AUGUSTINE
Rabbi Levi Vogel 904.521.8664

S. JOHNS
Rabbi Mendel Sharfstein 347.461.3765

SARASOTA
Rabbi Chaim Shaul Steinmetz 941.925.0770

SATELLITE BEACH
Rabbi Zvi Konikov 321.777.2770

SINGER ISLAND
Rabbi Berel Namdar 347.276.6985

SOUTH PALM BEACH
Rabbi Leibel Stolik 561.889.3499

SOUTH TAMPA
Rabbi Mendy Dubrowski 813.922.1723

SOUTHWEST BROWARD COUNTY
Rabbi Aryeh Schwartz 954.252.1770

SUNNY ISLES BEACH
Rabbi Alexander Kaller 305.803.5315

TAMARAC
Rabbi Kopel Silberberg 954.882.7434

WESLEY CHAPEL
Rabbi Mendy Yarmush
Rabbi Mendel Friedman 813.731.2977

WEST PALM BEACH
Rabbi Yoel Gancz 561.659.7770

WESTON
Rabbi Yisroel Spalter 954.349.6565

GEORGIA

ALPHARETTA
Rabbi Hirshy Minkowicz 770.410.9000

ATLANTA
Rabbi Yossi New
Rabbi Isser New 404.843.2464
Rabbi Alexander Piekarski 678.267.6418

ATLANTA: INTOWN
Rabbi Eliyahu Schusterman
Rabbi Ari Sollish 404.898.0434

CUMMING
Rabbi Levi Mentz 310.666.2218

GWINNETT
Rabbi Yossi Lerman 678.595.0196

MARIETTA
Rabbi Ephraim Silverman 770.565.4412

HAWAII

KAPA'A
Rabbi Michoel Goldman 808.647.4293

IDAHO

BOISE
Rabbi Mendel Lifshitz 208.853.9200

ILLINOIS

CHAMPAIGN
Rabbi Dovid Tiechtel 217.355.8672

CHICAGO
Rabbi Meir Hecht 312.714.4655
Rabbi Dovid Kotlarsky 773.495.7127
Rabbi Mordechai Gershon 773.412.5189
Rabbi Yosef Moscowitz 773.772.3770
Rabbi Levi Notik 773.274.5123

DES PLAINES
Rabbi Lazer Hershkovich 224.392.4442

ELGIN
Rabbi Mendel Shemtov 847.440.4486

GLENVIEW
Rabbi Yishaya Benjaminson 847.910.1738

HIGHLAND PARK
Mrs. Michla Schanowitz 847.266.0770

NORTHBROOK
Rabbi Meir Moscowitz 847.564.8770

OAK PARK
Rabbi Yitzchok Bergstein 708.524.1530

SKOKIE
Rabbi Yochanan Posner 847.677.1770

WILMETTE
Rabbi Dovid Flinkenstein 847.251.7707

INDIANA

INDIANAPOLIS
Rabbi Avraham Grossbaum
Rabbi Dr. Shmuel Klatzkin 317.251.5573

IOWA

BETTENDORF
Rabbi Shneur Cadaner 563.355.1065

KANSAS

OVERLAND PARK
Rabbi Mendy Wineberg 913.649.4852

KENTUCKY

LOUISVILLE
Rabbi Avrohom Litvin 502.459.1770

LOUISIANA

BATON ROUGE
Rabbi Peretz Kazen 225.267.7047

METAIRIE
Rabbi Yossie Nemes
Rabbi Mendel Ceitlin 504.454.2910

NEW ORLEANS
Rabbi Mendel Rivkin 504.302.1830

MAINE

PORTLAND
Rabbi Levi Wilansky 207.650.1783

MARYLAND

BALTIMORE
Rabbi Velvel Belinsky 410.764.5000
Classes in Russian

BEL AIR
Rabbi Kushi Schusterman 443.353.9718

BETHESDA
Rabbi Sender Geisinsky 301.913.9777

CHEVY CHASE
Rabbi Zalman Minkowitz 301.260.5000

COLUMBIA
Rabbi Hillel Baron
Rabbi Yosef Chaim Sufrin 410.740.2424

FREDERICK
Rabbi Boruch Labkowski 301.996.3659

GAITHERSBURG
Rabbi Sholom Raichik 301.926.3632

OLNEY
Rabbi Bentzy Stolik 301.660.6770

POTOMAC
Rabbi Mendel Bluming 301.983.4200
Rabbi Mendel Kaplan 301.983.1485

ROCKVILLE
Rabbi Shlomo Beitsh 646.773.2675
Rabbi Moishe Kavka 301.836.1242

MASSACHUSETTS

ANDOVER
Rabbi Asher Bronstein 978.470.2288

BOSTON
Rabbi Yosef Zaklos 617.297.7282

BRIGHTON
Rabbi Dan Rodkin 617.787.2200

CAPE COD
Rabbi Yekusiel Alperowitz 508.775.2324

LONGMEADOW

Rabbi Yakov Wolff 413.567.8665

NEWTON

Rabbi Shalom Ber Prus 617.244.1200

SUDBURY

Rabbi Yisroel Freeman 978.443.0110

SWAMPSCOTT

Rabbi Yossi Lipsker 781.581.3833

MICHIGAN

ANN ARBOR

Rabbi Aharon Goldstein 734.995.3276

BLOOMFIELD HILLS

Rabbi Levi Dubov 248.949.6210

GRAND RAPIDS

Rabbi Mordechai Haller 616.957.0770

WEST BLOOMFIELD

Rabbi Elimelech Silberberg 248.855.6170

MINNESOTA

MINNETONKA

Rabbi Mordechai Grossbaum
Rabbi Shmuel Silberstein 952.929.9922

S. PAUL

Rabbi Shneur Zalman Bendet 651.998.9298

MISSOURI

S. LOUIS

Rabbi Yosef Landa 314.725.0400

MONTANA

BOZEMAN

Rabbi Chaim Shaul Bruk 406.600.4934

NEVADA

LAS VEGAS

Rabbi Yosef Rivkin 702.217.2170

SUMMERLIN

Rabbi Yisroel Schanowitz
Rabbi Tzvi Bronchtain 702.855.0770

NEW JERSEY

BASKING RIDGE

Rabbi Mendy Herson
Rabbi Mendel Shemtov 908.604.8844

CHERRY HILL

Rabbi Mendel Mangel 856.874.1500

CLINTON

Rabbi Eli Kornfeld 908.623.7000

ENGLEWOOD

Rabbi Shmuel Konikov 201.519.7343

GREATER MERCER COUNTY

Rabbi Dovid Dubov
Rabbi Yaakov Chaiton 609.213.4136

HASKELL

Rabbi Mendy Gurkov 201.696.7609

HOLMDEL

Rabbi Shmaya Galperin 732.772.1998

MANALAPAN

Rabbi Boruch Chazanow
Rabbi Levi Wolosow 732.972.3687

MEDFORD

Rabbi Yitzchok Kahan 609.451.3522

MOUNTAIN LAKES

Rabbi Levi Dubinsky 973.551.1898

MULLICA HILL

Rabbi Avrohom Richler 856.733.0770

OLD TAPPAN

Rabbi Mendy Lewis 201.767.4008

RED BANK

Rabbi Dovid Harrison 718.915.8748

ROCKAWAY

Rabbi Asher Herson
Rabbi Mordechai Baumgarten 973.625.1525

RUTHERFORD

Rabbi Yitzchok Lerman 347.834.7500

SCOTCH PLAINS

Rabbi Avrohom Blesofsky 908.790.0008

SHORT HILLS

Rabbi Mendel Solomon
Rabbi Avrohom Levin 973.725.7008

SOUTH BRUNSWICK
Rabbi Levi Azimov 732.398.9492

TOMS RIVER
Rabbi Moshe Gourarie 732.349.4199

WEST ORANGE
Rabbi Mendy Kasowitz 973.325.6311

WOODCLIFF LAKE
Rabbi Dov Drizin 201.476.0157

NEW MEXICO

LAS CRUCES
Rabbi Bery Schmukler 575.524.1330

NEW YORK

BAY SHORE
Rabbi Shimon Stillerman 631.913.8770

BEDFORD
Rabbi Arik Wolf 914.666.6065

BINGHAMTON
Mrs. Rivkah Slonim 607.797.0015

BRIGHTON BEACH
Rabbi Moshe Winner 718.946.9833

BRONXVILLE
Rabbi Sruli Deitsch 917.755.0078

BROOKLYN
Rabbi Nissi Eber 347.677.2276
Rabbi Dovid Okonov 917.754.6942

BROOKVILLE
Rabbi Mendy Heber 516.626.0600

CEDARHURST
Rabbi Zalman Wolowik 516.295.2478

COMMACK
Rabbi Mendel Teldon 631.543.3343

DOBBS FERRY
Rabbi Benjy Silverman 914.693.6100

EAST HAMPTON
Rabbi Leibel Baumgarten
Rabbi Mendy Goldberg 631.329.5800

FOREST HILLS
Rabbi Yossi Mendelson 917.861.9726

GLEN OAKS
Rabbi Shmuel Nadler 347.388.7064

GREAT NECK
Rabbi Yoseph Geisinsky 516.487.4554

KINGSTON
Rabbi Yitzchok Hecht 845.334.9044

LARCHMONT
Rabbi Mendel Silberstein 914.834.4321

LITTLE NECK
Rabbi Eli Shifrin 718.423.1235

LONG BEACH
Rabbi Eli Goodman 516.574.3905

NEW HARTFORD
Rabbi Levi Charitonow 716.322.8692

MONTEBELLO
Rabbi Shmuel Gancz 845.746.1927

NEW YORK
Rabbi Shmuel Metzger 212.758.3770
Rabbi Mendy Weitman 917.232.7577
Mrs. Malka Werde 212.217.4148

NYC TRIBECA
Rabbi Zalman Paris 212.566.6764

NYC UPPER EAST SIDE
Rabbi Uriel Vigler 212.369.7310

OCEANSIDE
Rabbi Levi Gurkow 516.764.7385

OSSINING
Rabbi Dovid Labkowski 914.923.2522

OYSTER BAY
Rabbi Shmuel Lipszyc
Rabbi Shalom Lipszyc 347.853.9992

PARK SLOPE
Rabbi Menashe Wolf 347.957.1291

PORT WASHINGTON
Rabbi Shalom Paltiel 516.767.8672

PROSPECT HEIGHTS
Rabbi Mendy Hecht 347.622.3599

ROCHESTER
Rabbi Nechemia Vogel 585.271.0330

SOUTHAMPTON

Rabbi Chaim Pape 917.627.4865

STATEN ISLAND

Rabbi Mendy Katzman 718.370.8953

STONY BROOK

Rabbi Shalom Ber Cohen 631.585.0521

SUFFERN

Rabbi Shmuel Gancz 845.368.1889

NORTH CAROLINA

CARY

Rabbi Yisroel Cotlar 919.651.9710

CHARLOTTE

Rabbi Yossi Groner
Rabbi Shlomo Cohen 704.366.3984

GREENSBORO

Rabbi Yosef Plotkin 336.617.8120

RALEIGH

Rabbi Pinchas Herman
Rabbi Lev Cotlar 919.637.6950

OHIO

BEACHWOOD

Rabbi Shmuli Friedman 216.282.0112

CINCINNATI

Rabbi Yisroel Mangel 513.793.5200

COLUMBUS

Rabbi Yitzi Kaltmann 614.294.3296

DAYTON

Rabbi Nochum Mangel
Rabbi Shmuel Klatzkin 937.643.0770

OKLAHOMA

OKLAHOMA CITY

Rabbi Ovadia Goldman 405.524.4800

TULSA

Rabbi Yehuda Weg 918.492.4499

OREGON

PORTLAND

Rabbi Mordechai Wilhelm 503.977.9947

SALEM

Rabbi Avrohom Yitzchok Perlstein 503.383.9569

PENNSYLVANIA

AMBLER

Rabbi Shaya Deitsch 215.591.9310

BALA CYNWYD

Rabbi Shraga Sherman 610.660.9192

LAFAYETTE HILL

Rabbi Yisroel Kotlarsky 484.533.7009

MONROEVILLE

Rabbi Mendy Schapiro 412.372.1000

NEWTOWN

Rabbi Aryeh Weinstein 215.497.9925

PHILADELPHIA: CENTER CITY

Rabbi Yochonon Goldman 215.238.2100

PITTSBURGH

Rabbi Yisroel Altein 412.422.7300 EXT. 269

PITTSBURGH: SOUTH HILLS

Rabbi Mendy Rosenblum 412.278.3693

RYDAL

Rabbi Zushe Gurevitz 267.536.5757

UNIVERSITY PARK

Rabbi Nosson Meretsky 814.863.4929

WYNNEWOOD

Rabbi Moishe Brennan 610.529.9011

PUERTO RICO

CAROLINA

Rabbi Mendel Zarchi 787.253.0894

RHODE ISLAND

WARWICK

Rabbi Yossi Laufer 401.884.7888

SOUTH CAROLINA

COLUMBIA
Rabbi Hesh Epstein
Rabbi Levi Marrus 803.782.1831

TENNESSEE

KNOXVILLE
Rabbi Yossi Wilhelm 865.588.8584

MEMPHIS
Rabbi Levi Klein 901.754.0404

TEXAS

AUSTIN
Rabbi Mendy Levertov 512.905.2778

BELLAIRE
Rabbi Yossi Zaklikofsky 713.839.8887

DALLAS
Rabbi Mendel Dubrawsky
Rabbi Moshe Naparstek 972.818.0770

EL PASO
Rabbi Levi Greenberg 347.678.9762

FORT WORTH
Rabbi Dov Mandel 817.263.7701

HOUSTON
Rabbi Dovid Goldstein
Rabbi Zally Lazarus 281.589.7188
Rabbi Moishe Traxler 713.774.0300

HOUSTON: RICE UNIVERSITY AREA
Rabbi Eliezer Lazaroff 713.522.2004

LEAGUE CITY
Rabbi Yitzchok Schmukler 281.724.1554

PLANO
Rabbi Mendel Block
Rabbi Yehudah Horowitz 972.596.8270

S. ANTONIO
Rabbi Chaim Block
Rabbi Levi Teldon 210.492.1085
Rabbi Tal Shaul 210.877.4218

SOUTHLAKE
Rabbi Levi Gurevitch 817.451.1171

UTAH

SALT LAKE CITY
Rabbi Benny Zippel 801.467.7777

VERMONT

BURLINGTON
Rabbi Yitzchok Raskin 802.658.5770

MIDDLEBURY
Rabbi Binyamin Murray 802.578.2965

VIRGINIA

ALEXANDRIA/ARLINGTON
Rabbi Mordechai Newman 703.370.2774

FAIRFAX
Rabbi Leibel Fajnland 703.426.1980

GAINESVILLE
Rabbi Shmuel Perlstein 571.445.0342

LOUDOUN COUNTY
Rabbi Chaim Cohen 248.298.9279

NORFOLK
Rabbi Aaron Margolin
Rabbi Levi Brashevitzky 757.616.0770

RICHMOND
Rabbi Shlomo Pereira 804.740.2000

WASHINGTON

BELLINGHAM
Rabbi Yosef Truxton 360.224.9919

MERCER ISLAND
Rabbi Elazar Bogomilsky 206.527.1411
Rabbi Nissan Kornfeld 206.851.2324

OLYMPIA
Rabbi Yosef Schtroks 360.867.8804

SEATTLE
Rabbi Yoni Levitin 206.851.9831
Rabbi Shnai Levitin 347.342.2259

SPOKANE COUNTY
Rabbi Yisroel Hahn 509.443.0770

WISCONSIN

BAYSIDE

Rabbi Cheski Edelman 414.439.5041

MEQUON

Rabbi Menachem Rapoport 262.242.2235

MILWAUKEE

Rabbi Levi Emmer 414.277.8839

Rabbi Mendel Shmotkin 414.961.6100

ARGENTINA

BUENOS AIRES

Mrs. Chani Gorowitz 54.11.4865.0445

Rabbi Menachem M. Grunblatt 54.911.3574.0037

Rabbi Mendy Gurevitch 55.11.4545.7771

Rabbi Shlomo Levy 54.11.4807.2223

Rabbi Yosef Levy 54.11.4504.1908

Rabbi Mendi Mizrahi 54.11.4963.1221

Rabbi Shiele Plotka 54.11.4634.3111

Rabbi Pinhas Sudry 54.1.4822.2285

Rabbi Shloimi Setton 54.11.4982.8637

CORDOBA

Rabbi Menajem Turk 54.351.233.8250

SALTA

Rabbi Rafael Tawil 54.387.421.4947

S. MIGUEL DE TUCUMÁN

Rabbi Ariel Levy 54.381.473.6944

AUSTRALIA

NEW SOUTH WALES

DOUBLE BAY

Rabbi Yanky Berger 612.9327.1644

DOVER HEIGHTS

Rabbi Motti Feldman 614.0400.8572

NORTH SHORE

Rabbi Nochum Schapiro

Rebbetzin Fruma Schapiro 612.9488.9548

QUEENSLAND

BRISBANE

Rabbi Levi Jaffe 617.3843.6770

VICTORIA

BRIGHTON

Rabbi Levi Kurinsky 613.9994.5611

MOORABBIN

Rabbi Elisha Greenbaum 614.0349.0434

WESTERN AUSTRALIA

PERTH

Rabbi Shalom White 618.9275.2106

AZERBAIJAN

BAKU

Mrs. Chavi Segal 994.12.597.91.90

BELARUS

BOBRUISK

Mrs. Mina Hababo 375.29.104.3230

MINSK

Rabbi Shneur Deitsch

Mrs. Bassie Deitsch 375.29.330.6675

BELGIUM

BRUSSELS

Rabbi Shmuel Pinson 375.29.330.6675

BRAZIL

CURITIBA

Rabbi Mendy Labkowski 55.41.3079.1338

S. PAULO

Rabbi Avraham Steinmetz 55.11.3081.3081

CANADA

ALBERTA

CALGARY

Rabbi Mordechai Groner 403.281.3770

EDMONTON

Rabbi Ari Drelich

Rabbi Mendy Blachman 780.200.5770

BRITISH COLUMBIA

KELOWNA
Rabbi Shmuly Hecht 250.575.5384

RICHMOND
Rabbi Yechiel Baitelman 604.277.6427

VANCOUVER
Rabbi Dovid Rosenfeld 604.266.1313

VICTORIA
Rabbi Meir Kaplan 250.595.7656

MANITOBA

WINNIPEG
Rabbi Shmuel Altein 204.339.8737

ONTARIO

MAPLE
Rabbi Yechezkel Deren 647.883.6372

MISSISSAUGA
Rabbi Yitzchok Slavin 905.820.4432

OTTAWA
Rabbi Menachem M. Blum 613.843.7770

THORNHILL
Rabbi Yisroel Landa 416.897.3338

GREATER TORONTO REGIONAL OFFICE & THORNHILL
Rabbi Yossi Gansburg 905.731.7000

TORONTO
Rabbi Shmuel Neft 647.966.7105

WATERLOO
Rabbi Moshe Goldman 226.338.7770

QUEBEC

CÔTE S.-LUC
Rabbi Levi Naparstek 438.409.6770

DOLLARD-DES ORMEAUX
Rabbi Leibel Fine 514.777.4675

HAMPSTEAD
Rabbi Moshe New
Rabbi Berel Bell 514.739.0770

MONTREAL
Rabbi Ronnie Fine
Pesach Nussbaum 514.738.3434

OLD MONTREAL/GRIFFINTOWN
Rabbi Nissan Gansbourg
Rabbi Berel Bell 514.800.6966

S. LAZARE
Rabbi Nochum Labkowski 514.436.7426

TOWN OF MOUNT ROYAL
Rabbi Moshe Krasnanski
Rabbi Shneur Zalman Rader 514.342.1770

SASKATCHEWAN

SASKATOON
Rabbi Raphael Kats 306.384.4370

COLOMBIA

BOGOTA
Rabbi Chanoch Piekarski 57.1.635.8251

COSTA RICA

S. JOSÉ
Rabbi Hershel Spalter
Rabbi Moshe Bitton 506.4010.1515

CROATIA

ZAGREB
Rabbi Pinchas Zaklas 385.1.4812227

DENMARK

COPENHAGEN
Rabbi Yitzchok Loewenthal 45.3316.1850

DOMINICAN REPUBLIC

S. DOMINGO
Rabbi Shimon Pelman 829.341.2770

ESTONIA

TALLINN
Rabbi Shmuel Kot 372.662.30.50

FRANCE

BOULOGNE
Rabbi Michael Sojcher 33.1.46.99.87.85

DIJON
Rabbi Chaim Slonim 33.6.52.05.26.65

LA VARENNE-S.-HILAIRE
Rabbi Mena'hem Mendel Benelbaz 33.6.17.81.57.47

MARSEILLE
Rabbi Eliahou Altabe 33.6.11.60.03.05
Rabbi Mena'hem Mendel Assouline 33.6.64.88.25.04
Rabbi Emmanuel Taubenblatt 33.4.88.00.94.85

PARIS
Rabbi Yona Hasky 33.1.53.75.36.01
Rabbi Acher Marciano 33.6.15.15.01.02
Rabbi Avraham Barou'h Pevzner 33.6.99.64.07.70

PONTAULT-COMBAULT
Rabbi Yossi Amar 33.6.61.36.07.70

VILLIERS-SUR-MARNE
Rabbi Mena'hem Mendel Mergui 33.1.49.30.89.66

GEORGIA

TBILISI
Rabbi Meir Kozlovsky 995.32.2429770

GERMANY

BERLIN
Rabbi Yehuda Tiechtel 49.30.2128.0830

DUSSELDORF
Rabbi Chaim Barkahn 49.173.2871.770

HAMBURG
Rabbi Shlomo Bistritzky 49.40.4142.4190

HANNOVER 49.511.811.2822
Chapter founded by Rabbi Binyamin Wolff, OBM

GREECE

ATHENS
Rabbi Mendel Hendel 30.210.323.3825

GUATEMALA

GUATEMALA CITY
Rabbi Shalom Pelman 502.2485.0770

ISRAEL

ASHKELON
Rabbi Shneor Lieberman 054.977.0512

BALFURYA
Rabbi Noam Bar-Tov 054.580.4770

CAESAREA
Rabbi Chaim Meir Lieberman 054.621.2586

EVEN YEHUDA
Rabbi Menachem Noyman 054.777.0707

GANEI TIKVA
Rabbi Gershon Shnur 054.524.2358

GIV'ATAYIM
Rabbi Pinchus Bitton 052.643.8770

JERUSALEM
Rabbi Levi Diamond 055.665.7702
Rabbi Avraham Hendel 054.830.5799

KARMIEL
Rabbi Mendy Elishevitz 054.521.3073

KFAR SABA
Rabbi Yossi Baitch 054.445.5020

KIRYAT BIALIK
Rabbi Pinny Marton 050.661.1768

KIRYAT MOTZKIN
Rabbi Shimon Eizenbach 050.902.0770

KOCHAV YAIR
Rabbi Dovi Greenberg 054.332.6244

MACCABIM-RE'UT
Rabbi Yosef Yitzchak Noiman 054.977.0549

NES ZIYONA
Rabbi Menachem Feldman 054.497.7092

NETANYA
Rabbi Schneur Brod 054.579.7572

RAMAT GAN-KRINITZI
Rabbi Yisroel Gurevitz 052.743.2814

RAMAT GAN-MAROM NAVE
Rabbi Binyamin Meir Kali 050.476.0770

RAMAT YISHAI
Rabbi Shneor Zalman Wolosow 052.324.5475

RISHON LEZION
Rabbi Uri Keshet 050.722.4593

ROSH PINA
Rabbi Sholom Ber Hertzel 052.458.7600

TEL AVIV
Rabbi Shneur Piekarski 054.971.5568

JAPAN

TOKYO
Rabbi Mendi Sudakevich 81.3.5789.2846

KAZAKHSTAN

ALMATY
Rabbi Shevach Zlatopolsky 7.7272.77.59.49

KYRGYZSTAN

BISHKEK
Rabbi Arye Raichman 996.312.68.19.66

LATVIA

RIGA
Rabbi Shneur Zalman Kot
Mrs. Rivka Glazman 371.6720.40.22

LITHUANIA

VILNIUS
Rabbi Sholom Ber Krinsky 370.6817.1367

LUXEMBOURG

LUXEMBOURG
Rabbi Mendel Edelman 352.2877.7079

NETHERLANDS

ALMERE
Rabbi Moshe Stiefel 31.36.744.0509

AMSTERDAM
Rabbi Yanki Jacobs 31.644.988.627
Rabbi Jaacov Zwi Spiero 31.652.328.065

EINDHOVEN
Rabbi Simcha Steinberg 31.63.635.7593

HAGUE
Rabbi Shmuel Katzman 31.70.347.0222

HEEMSTEDE-HAARLEM
Rabbi Shmuel Spiero 31.23.532.0707

MAASTRICHT
Rabbi Avrohom Cohen 32.48.549.6766

NIJMEGEN
Rabbi Menachem Mendel Levine 31.621.586.575

ROTTERDAM
Rabbi Yehuda Vorst 31.10.265.5530

PANAMA

PANAMA CITY
Rabbi Ari Laine
Rabbi Gabriel Benayon 507.223.3383

RUSSIA

ASTRAKHAN
Rabbi Yisroel Melamed 7.851.239.28.24

BRYANSK
Rabbi Menachem Mendel Zaklas 7.483.264.55.15

CHELYABINSK
Rabbi Meir Kirsh 7.351.263.24.68

MOSCOW
Rabbi Aizik Rosenfeld 7.906.762.88.81
Rabbi Mordechai Weisberg 7.495.645.50.00

NIZHNY NOVGOROD
Rabbi Shimon Bergman 7.920.253.47.70

NOVOSIBIRSK
Rabbi Shneur Zalmen Zaklos 7.903.900.43.22

OMSK
Rabbi Osher Krichevsky 7.381.231.33.07

PERM
Rabbi Zalman Deutch 7.342.212.47.32

ROSTOV
Rabbi Chaim Danzinger 7.8632.99.02.68

S. PETERSBURG
Rabbi Shalom Pewzner 7.911.726.21.19
Rabbi Zvi Pinsky 7.812.713.62.09

SAMARA
Rabbi Shlomo Deutch 7.846.333.40.64

SARATOV
Rabbi Yaakov Kubitshek 7.8452.21.58.00

TOGLIATTI
Rabbi Meier Fischer 7.848.273.02.84

UFA
Rabbi Dan Krichevsky 7.347.244.55.33

VORONEZH
Rabbi Levi Stiefel 7.473.252.96.99

SINGAPORE

SINGAPORE
Rabbi Mordechai Abergel 656.337.2189
Rabbi Netanel Rivni 656.336.2127
Classes in Hebrew

SOUTH AFRICA

JOHANNESBURG
Rabbi Dovid Masinter
Rabbi Ari Kievman 27.11.440.6600

SWITZERLAND

LUZERN
Rabbi Chaim Drukman 41.41.361.1770

THAILAND

BANGKOK
Rabbi Yosef C. Kantor 6681.837.7618

UKRAINE

BERDITCHEV
Mrs. Chana Thaler 380.637.70.37.70

DNEPROPETROVSK
Rabbi Dan Makagon 380.504.51.13.18

NIKOLAYEV
Rabbi Sholom Gotlieb 380.512.37.37.71

ODESSA
Rabbi Avraham Wolf
Rabbi Yaakov Neiman 38.048.728.0770 EXT. 280

ZAPOROZHYE
Mrs. Nechama Dina Ehrentreu 380.957.19.96.08

ZHITOMIR
Rabbi Shlomo Wilhelm 380.504.63.01.32

UNITED KINGDOM

BOURNEMOUTH
Rabbi Bentzion Alperowitz 44.749.456.7177

CHEADLE
Rabbi Peretz Chein 44.161.428.1818

LEEDS
Rabbi Eli Pink 44.113.266.3311

LONDON
Rabbi Moshe Adler 44.771.052.4460
Rabbi Mendel Cohen 44.777.261.2661
Rabbi Shneor Glitzenstein 44.792.585.7050
Rabbi Hillel Gruber 44.208.202.1600
Rabbi Chaim Hoch 44.753.879.9524
Rabbi Dovid Katz 44.207.624.2770
Rabbi Eli Levin 44.7540.461.568
Rabbi Yisroel Lew 44.207.060.9770
Rabbi Yossi Simon 44.208.458.0416
Rabbi Shneur Wineberg 44.745.628.6538

MANCHESTER
Rabbi Levi Cohen 44.161.792.6335
Rabbi Shmuli Jaffe 44.161.766.1812

RADLETT, HERTFORDSHIRE
Rabbi Alexander Sender Dubrawsky 44.79.4380.8965

The Jewish Learning Multiplex

Brought to you by the Rohr Jewish Learning Institute

In fulfillment of the mandate of the Lubavitcher Rebbe, of blessed memory, whose leadership guides every step of our work, the mission of the Rohr Jewish Learning Institute is to transform Jewish life and the greater community through the study of Torah, connecting each Jew to our shared heritage of Jewish learning.

While our flagship program remains the cornerstone of our organization, JLI is proud to feature additional divisions catering to specific populations, in order to meet a wide array of educational needs.

THE ROHR JEWISH LEARNING INSTITUTE

A subsidiary of Merkos L'Inyonei Chinuch,
the adult educational arm of the Chabad-Lubavitch movement

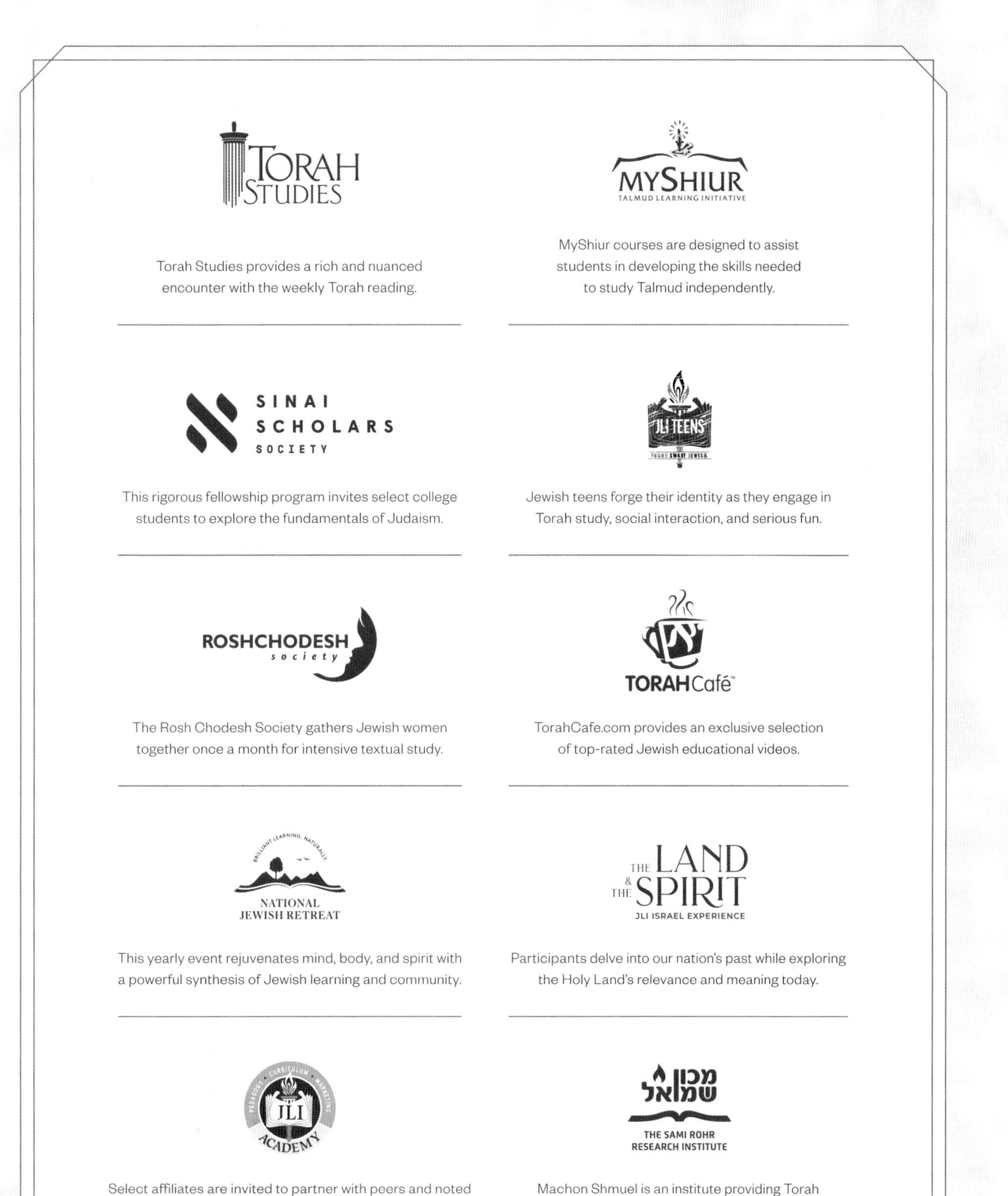

TORAH STUDIES
Torah Studies provides a rich and nuanced encounter with the weekly Torah reading.
MYSHIUR
TALMUD LEARNING INITIATIVE
MyShiur courses are designed to assist students in developing the skills needed to study Talmud independently.
SINAI SCHOLARS SOCIETY
This rigorous fellowship program invites select college students to explore the fundamentals of Judaism.
JLI TEENS
Jewish teens forge their identity as they engage in Torah study, social interaction, and serious fun.
ROSHCHODESH society
The Rosh Chodesh Society gathers Jewish women together once a month for intensive textual study.
TORAH Café
TorahCafe.com provides an exclusive selection of top-rated Jewish educational videos.
BRILLIANT LEARNING. NATURALLY.
NATIONAL JEWISH RETREAT
This yearly event rejuvenates mind, body, and spirit with a powerful synthesis of Jewish learning and community.
THE LAND & THE SPIRIT
JLI ISRAEL EXPERIENCE
Participants delve into our nation's past while exploring the Holy Land's relevance and meaning today.
PEDAGOGY · CURRICULUM · MARKETING
JLI ACADEMY
Select affiliates are invited to partner with peers and noted professionals, as leaders of innovation and excellence.
מכון שמואל
THE SAMI ROHR RESEARCH INSTITUTE
Machon Shmuel is an institute providing Torah research in the service of educators worldwide.

NOTES